HOW-TO-DO-IT

UPHOLSTERING

and

RE-UPHOLSTERING

Incorporating the newest materials with the latest methods of procedure, this book simplifies the art, making it understandable and approachable for the amateur as well as keeping the professional up-to-date. All types of furniture and all types of problems are clearly illustrated and explained.

by

CLYDE AGNEW CRISWELL

Fully Illustrated

Illustrations by Wally Bieger

CHICAGO, ILLINOIS

FREDERICK J. DRAKE & CO.

Publishers

Printed in the United States of America

INTRODUCTION:

As it is with many of the skilled crafts and trades, so it is with upholstery. Throughout the years upholstery has gone from simply the barest sort of pad for comfort to the plush overstuffed furniture. In the beginning solid comfort meant just that with the medieval chair or bench, unadorned by cloth. As time went on the furniture took on a more complicated aspect. The craft took on more mystery until today we approach a finely upholstered chair with near reverence and mystification. There will not be a word said to deny the skill of a practiced upholstery artist. Many jobs are wiser deferred to the upholstery shop and the already skilled. In this book I have made an effort to make the art understandable and approachable. There is no crying necessity to bring "How-To-Upholster" to every home, nor close the professional shop. If anything, one excursion into the field of "do-it-yourself" will give you a view of the problems which beset the professional. If you are successful, you both will profit indirectly: you by your industry and success, and he by your advertising the art as practiced by the skilled. In this book you will find the basic construction of furniture treated rather superficially, the complete repadding of the piece somewhat better covered, and the major part of the description concerned with reupholstering: covering, rewebbing, and reshaping of ornamentation, the things most likely to concern the beginner.

Larger projects are sometimes easier to complete with the professional look. The smaller job will involve less work and less cost, to be sure, but the workmanship on a smaller piece must stand closer scrutiny. Mistakes often can be covered or ignored on the larger but must be corrected on the smaller. If you have a project, jump in with hammer and tacks and forethought, all equally important. I cannot emphasize strongly enough the importance of carefully noting how the job was done originally; careful notation is extremely important for future reference when the time comes to replace old material with the new. In reupholstery jobs a single reading of any book cannot give you all the answers. Much additional help will come from the knowledge of the way it was done before.

TABLE OF CONTENTS

INTRODUCTION

Chapter 1

Chapter 2

Chapter 3

Chapter 4

Chapter 5

Chapter 6

Chapter 7

Chapter 8

Chapter 9

Chapter 10

Chapter 1

MATERIALS

Many of the materials and methods of upholstery have remained the same over the last one hundred years. During the last ten years new methods have been developed in upholstery work through new materials devised for other industries. These new inventions in materials and methods have brought to the trade sagless spring wire supports, torsion springs, the companion of both and the formed spring wire edging. A completely new all-in-one cushioning and resilient material for upholstery padding was developed out of foam rubber. The padding fibers formerly used in all stuffing and forming work (cotton, animal hair, vegetable fibers) have been combined with either plastic or rubber material, producing a superior upholstery element. This rubberized fiber resists and in most cases defies rodents, moths, mildew, and vermin. Its increased weight is offset by its added resilience and the fact that less material is required for the same job.

These new materials and their applications have in many cases reduced the overall cost of good furniture, and in cases of reupholstery, have cut the labor time of renovation in half. The most interesting factor in these new elements is the ease with which they can be used by the amateur and professional alike. The chief drawback lies in the necessity for special tools and the knowledge of the proper application of these new materials. As in the case of foam rubber, it is not the best material for a job involving moisture and poor air circulation. In this case the sagless spring and the formed wire edge without excessive organic padding would prove in time to be more satisfactory. These substitutions will be discussed in full as the text progresses. The actual methods of application will be discussed as a need appears for the new material in one of the projects.

9

The sagless (zig-zag) spring wire has been used for some time with great success. However, it is of prime importance that the proper spring strength be chosen. The physical dimensions of the unit on which the sagless spring is to be

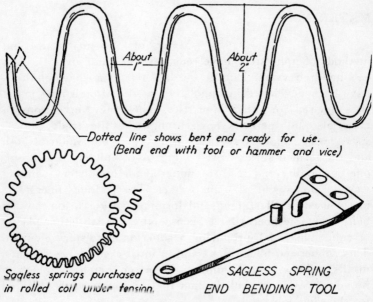

Figure 1—Sagless Springs

applied, the probable weight of the load, the length of the span and the strength of the fastening edges must be considered.

The sagless spring (Fig. 1) is commercially produced in many gauge sizes for the two major applications, backs and seats. When this sagless spring wire is purchased it comes in coiled up form like a garden hose. It is sometimes under tension like a clock spring and can cause injury if not handled carefully. The action of this spring when it is applied to the frame performs the service of support in constantly trying to regain its coiled form. Because of the variety of furniture frames, a number of styles of metal retaining clips, as shown in Fig. 2, have been designed to hold the sagless spring wire ends. These clips have been standardized into four types: the

C, E, G, and K clips, each for a different job. The C clip is for seat back rails or where nailing cannot be easily performed. The E clip is a three nail clip for heavy duty supporting, simi-

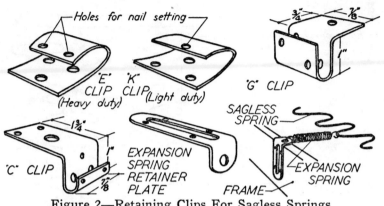

Figure 2—Retaining Clips For Sagless Springs

lar in size to the K clip for average duty. The G clip is used for top and outside surfaces where the springs should be recessed inside the frame for concealment. Since the sagless spring wire tends to bow up, it is often desirable to increase the

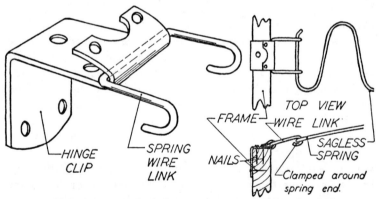

Figure 3—Hinge Clips and Wire Hinge Links

amount of bowing for more comfort. In these cases the hinge clip can be used to advantage. Hinge clips come with a hinge link of bent wire (Fig. 3) which will add this extended bow to the sagless spring. Additional accessories to the sagless

spring are the expansion coil springs used as tie-ins between
the lengths of sagless spring and the boundary frame members
(Fig. 4). These give the overall spring effect rather than hav-

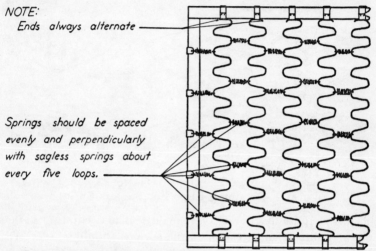

NOTE:
Ends always alternate ————

Springs should be spaced
evenly and perpendicularly
with sagless springs about
every five loops. ————

Figure 4—Application of Expansion Coil Springs With
Sagless Spring

ing each length act as its own section. These extension helical
springs can be purchased in different sizes, according to the
expected load. In planning which type to use, consider that it
is best to use the extended spring for lighter loads in the back
sagless units and the non-extended spring for the seats and
heavily loaded areas.

Edge or cushion boundary wire is usually spring steel of
exceptional strength. It is purchased in ten foot lengths and
in gauges (diameters) from #9 to #14 (#9 is the heavier
wire.) Seats require heavier gauge boundary wire than the
backs or other formed sections. These border or boundary
wires are supported by edge springs (Fig. 5) which are in
turn fastened to the sagless spring wires. Formerly, these two
members were fastened by steel wire wrappings which wore
out in time. It is now possible to use especially prepared clips
which bind these two, the edge wire and the edge springs
together.

The torsion spring illustrated in Fig. 6 has been designed
to keep the corner construction of the back or seat firm. It is

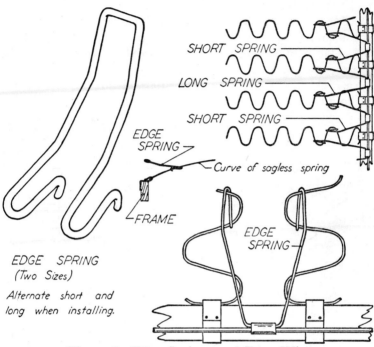

SHORT SPRING

LONG SPRING

SHORT SPRING

EDGE SPRING

Curve of sagless spring

FRAME

EDGE SPRING

EDGE SPRING
(Two Sizes)

Alternate short and
long when installing.

Figure 5—Edge Springs and Edge Wire

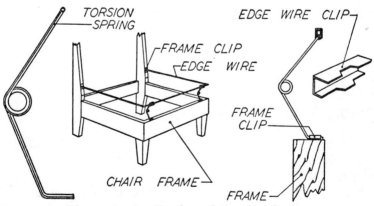

TORSION SPRING

EDGE WIRE CLIP

FRAME CLIP

EDGE WIRE

FRAME CLIP

CHAIR FRAME

FRAME

Figure 6—Application of Torsion Spring

supported on the frame and is clipped to the edge wire. As this section is depressed, the spring folds in tension and tends to resist the weight.

Recently a completely pre-formed cushion or back wire spring unit as shown in Fig. 7 has come on the market. It is possible to obtain this unit in many standard sizes and shapes. It comes assembled and ready to be fastened in place by the spring clips, over the standard jute webbing or steel strap webbing.

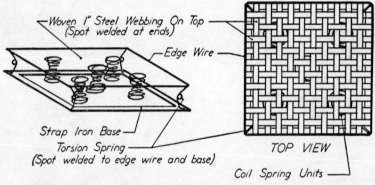

Figure 7—Pre-Made Spring Units

Steel strap webbing has become the standard repair and replacement webbing for old furniture units. It can be applied to most any type of unit and will give permanent support to

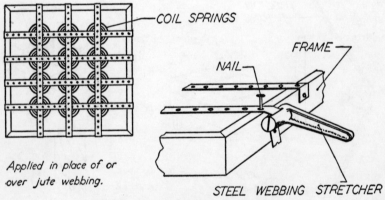

Figure 8—Steel Strap Webbing

the springing. This material can be purchased at any hardware store, and is frequently used in the plumbing and carpentry trades. It is necessary to acquire a special stretching tool, as illustrated in Fig. 8, for the application of the steel strapping.

When the steel spring work has been constructed, there is a group of padding materials which are easier to handle and require somewhat less than professional skill to apply. The rubberized fibers (both man-made and natural organic fibers) are used. This fiber comes either in the form of block fiber in

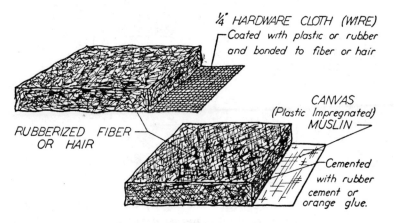

Figure 9—Rubberized Fiber or Hair With Backing

many thicknesses or in the same shape but with a special wire reinforced backing. Where these fiber pads must be used to form a soft curved shape, they may be obtained with a canvas back, vulcanized in place (see Fig. 9). The home craftsman can often effect this same backing with rubber cement and the fiber material of his choosing.

The wire and cloth woven "insulator" has made its way into the upholstery field since it makes possible a great saving in padding costs (foam rubber or fiber). The term "insulator" derives from the fact that it eliminates any chance of the springs being felt through the thin padding. This insulator, shown in Fig. 10, consists of spring wire woven into a canvas or burlap cloth. The wire, spaced about one inch apart, forms

a platform for the springs to push against. It can be purchased
in rolls in many widths and lengths.

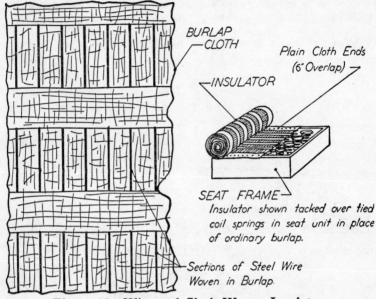

BURLAP
CLOTH

Plain Cloth Ends
(6" Overlap)

INSULATOR

SEAT FRAME
Insulator shown tacked over tied
coil springs in seat unit in place
of ordinary burlap.

Sections of Steel Wire
Woven in Burlap.

Figure 10—Wire and Cloth Woven Insulator

In doing any work with these highly tempered spring steel
products a word of caution is necessary since the loose end of
any piece of spring can easily fly up too fast to be ducked. An
injured or blinded eye can result.

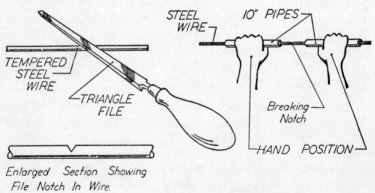

STEEL
WIRE

10" PIPES

TEMPERED
STEEL
WIRE

TRIANGLE
FILE

Breaking
Notch

HAND POSITION

Enlarged Section Showing
File Notch In Wire.

Figure 11—Breaking Steel Wire

There are special tools such as the steel webbing stretcher, the edge wire bending pipe, and the cutting file. Since an ordinary pair of pliers cannot cut this tempered steel, a necking triangle file forms a necessary part of your equipment. A small file cut part-way through the wire and the use of the bending pipe will allow you to break the wire wherever you wish (see Fig. 11). Do not try to cut this material with side cutting

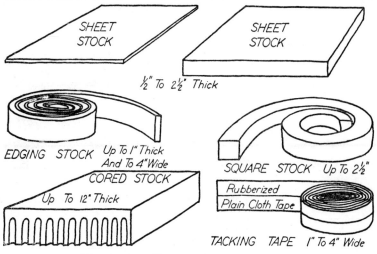

Figure 12—Types of Foam Rubber

pliers or tin shears, as the blades of these tools are not designed for such hard material and can be easily damaged. Heating and soldering or welding is not advised unless you are familiar with the precise process of tempering the wire again. For the layman this is virtually impossible.

Foam rubber is somewhat easier to handle since it can be purchased in most any size you desire, either in solid or cored stock (round holes reducing the mass of the rubber unit) as shown in Fig. 12. These different types of stock will be found in different densities for different loads. These compression densities range from 10 to 100 pounds.

This material is readily fashioned and fabricated into whatever shape you desire. The manufacturers have marketed allied materials such as binding tape (rubberized), tacking tape (half rubberized), rubber cement, and cutting tools. A long breadknife with a serrated edge, or a fine tooth band saw will do an excellent job. The use of tailors shears is left to the professional. However, some trimming will be necessary in any event.

There is on the market a foam rubber covered air pocket in standard cushion sizes (see Fig. 13). This trapped air gives less weight and cost to the equivalent size unit. It must be treated with care to avoid being punctured.

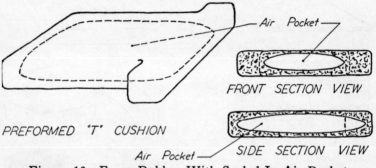

PREFORMED "T" CUSHION

Air Pocket — FRONT SECTION VIEW

Air Pocket — SIDE SECTION VIEW

Figure 13—Foam Rubber With Sealed-In Air Pocket

When the foam rubber is being handled in any particular application the use of soapstone powder will decrease surface friction. This powder can be applied to the tools or to the foam rubber (where excess cement has been used).

Coated fibers have now taken the place of the older and more difficult to handle loose fibers or hair understuffing. As these new padding materials are not pliable enough for curved surfaces and do not bend evenly, it is often impractical to use them under stuffing. There are several different types of fibers which can be obtained in pad form, all coated with natural or neoprene rubber. There is little difference, and if any, it is in favor of the synthetic rubber. The pads come in several thicknesses and have different resiliencies, depending upon their density. Some of these pads, as it was mentioned earlier, have commercial backing of hardware cloth or heavy canvas (both cemented in place). Regardless of the type of pad, care must be exercised in cutting. Small, light, stroking cuts do less crushing damage to the fibers. A very sharp knife or shears

should be employed. When it is necessary to fit two sections
together for a large area of padding, either for surface area or
for depth, the pads can be cemented together, and where several layers are to be glued up, the denser pads are used in the
lower layer. When the pads are tacked to the frame, it is wise
to use large headed upholstery tacks, pounding them into the
fiber with about ¼ of the thickness under the tack head. The
hole can be pulled together to cover the head. In all cases the
coated fibers must be covered with a layer of upholstery
cotton (Egyptian or moss cotton) or with ½″ to 1″ of
foam rubber.

In preparing for the application of the sagless springs, the
framing of the particular piece of furniture must be checked
and strengthened wherever necessary. For loading strength
and spring wire size refer to tables listed toward the end of
this chapter.

Glue is often needed in the renovation or reupholstery of
old pieces of furniture. Since World War II the polyvinyl
glues have come into use. They are exceptionally strong and
require little or no clamping pressure. However, there are
some on the market which are not suitable for furniture work
(due to thinning or improper mixture by the manufacturer).
Regardless of the brand, glue must be fresh. Never use white
vinyl glue which has jelled.

Wire Gauge for Sagless Springs Used in Backs

Length of spring shown is from bottom to top of back. The
smaller the gauge number, the larger and stronger the sagless
spring wire.

Spring Length (Inside)	Sagless Springs Gauge	Spring Length (Inside)	Sagless Springs Gauge
18″	12½ ga.	26″	11 ga.
19″	12½ ga.	27″	11 ga.
20″	12 ga.	28″	10 ga.
21″	12 ga.	29″	10 ga.
22″	12 ga.	30″	10 ga.
23″	12 ga.	33″	10 ga.
24″	11 ga.	36″	9 ga.
25″	11 ga.	40″	9 ga.

How to Choose the Correct Number and Size Sagless Springs

Furniture piece (inside front rail)	Number of sagless springs (run from Front-back)	Clip spacing (measured on center)	Spacing of end clips	Connecting helical and/or extension spring size
15″	4	about 3″	1″	None (or special)
16″	4	about 3″	1″	Same
17″	4	about 3″	1″	Same
18″	4	about 3½″	1¼″	Same
19″	4 or 5	about 3½″	1¼″	1½″
20″	5	about 4″	1½″	1¾″
21″	5	about 4″	1¾″	1¾″
22″	5	4½″	2″	2″
23″	5	about 4½″	2″	3″
24″	5 or 6	between 5″/4″	2″	2″
25″	6	4½″	1½″	2″
26″	6	about 4½″	1¾″	2″
30″	7	about 4″	1½″	2″
36″	8	about 4¼″	1¾″	3″
40″	9	about 4¾″	2″	3″
48″	10	about 5″	2″	3″
58″	12	about 5″	1½″	3″
59″	12	5″	2″	3″
60″	13	4¾″	1½″	3″
61″	13	4¾″	2″	3″
63″	13	5″	1½″	3″
65″	14	4¾″	1½″	3″
67″	15	4½″	2″	2″

Smaller than 15 inch seats or backs do not warrant sagless springs or wire forming unless a special case arises.

In applying the sagless springs to any back section it must be remembered that less weight is placed against the back section of the springs. The sagless springs run from top to bottom and may be curved into a design ordinarily impossible with seating areas. The degree of curve is governed from bottom to top frame member or from the front to back frame member of the seat, and it is this measurement that must be used. If simply a normal seat or back curve is desired, then subtract the length of the clip from each end of the sagless spring, or approximately one half inch at each end (one inch

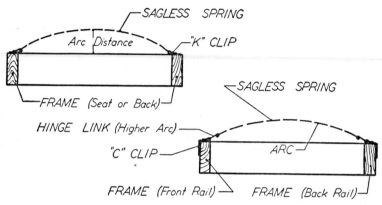

Figure 14—Sagless Spring Surface Arcs

less than the direct measurement overall). The following table will give the measurements for most any seat or back depth and several measurements of surface curves (Arcs) described in Fig. 14.

Seat and Back Measurements
With Various Curve Measurements

Between Frame Rail Measurement	Sagless Spring Wire Gauge	Curves or Arcs (Adaptions are possible with care in measurement and framing)				
		1″	1¼″	1½″	1¾″	2″
10″ to 11″	12 ga.	9½″- 10½″	9¾″- 10¾″	10″- 11″	10½″- 11½″	Not used
12″	11 ga.	11½″	11¾″	12″	12½″	Not used
13″	11 ga.	12½″	12¾″	13″	13½″	Not used
14″	11 ga.	13½″	13¾″	14″	14½″	Not used
15″	10 ga.	14½″	14¾″	15″	15½″	Not used

(Continued next page)

Seat and Back Measurements
With Various Curve Measurements

(Continued from preceding page)

Between Frame Rail Measurement	Sagless Spring Wire Gauge	Curves or Arcs (Adaptions are possible with care in measurement and framing)				
		1″	1¼″	1½″	1¾″	2″
16″	10 ga.	15¼″	15¾″	16″	16¼″	Not used
17″	10 ga.	16″	16½″	16¼″	17″	Not used
18″	10 ga.	16¾″	17¼″	17½″	18″	Not used
19″	9 ga.	17¾″	18¼″	18½″	18¾″	19″
20″	9 ga.	18¾″	19¼″	19½″	19¾″	20″
21″	9 ga.	19¾″	20″	20½″	20¾″	21″
22″	9 ga.	20¾″	21″	21½″	21¾″	22″
23″	8 ga.	21¾″	22″	22½″	22¾″	23″
24″	8 ga.	22¾″	23″	23½″	23¾″	24″
25″	8 ga.	23¾″	24″	24½″	24¾″	25″
26″	8 ga.	24¾″	25″	25½″	25¾″	26″
27″	8 ga.	25¾″	26″	26¼″	26½″	27″
28″ to 30″	8 ga.	26¾″ to 28¾″	27″ to 29″	27¼″ to 29¼″	27½″ to 29½″	28″ to 30″

In this chapter we have discussed the most important new
materials and methods now used by the professional. Further
on in the book the exact techniques involved will come to
light in the various projects described. There will be further
illustrations of the applications of these new materials and
more explanation. This chapter was inserted only to give you
an idea of what can be done. I have not intended to suggest
that this type of upholstery has supplanted the older but still
adequate materials.

In reupholstery there is often a chance to use new materials
with a considerable saving and a minimum of work. Care
must be taken to see that the frame of the old piece will stand
the stress of the sagless springs or the steel webbing.

Chapter 2

TOOLS AND PREPARATIONS

As in doing any job there are certain preparatory elements which have to be considered. Chances are that without much effort these preparations can

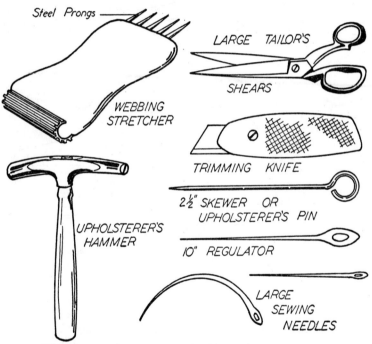

Figure 15—Tools—General Types Most Needed

be satisfied without much effort in the average home work shop or tool drawer. The amount and type of tools, the place where you will work, proper lighting, and some sort of soft non-scratching surface on which to work, are the conditions of the greatest importance.

23

Tools—Consider the matter of tools first, since you can really work about anywhere and on anything depending upon how particular you are. (See Fig. 15 for general tools.) First is the tack hammer (with one end magnetized for holding tacks, preferably, although any hammer will do). Other necessary tools, as illustrated in Figs. 15 and 16, are the fol-

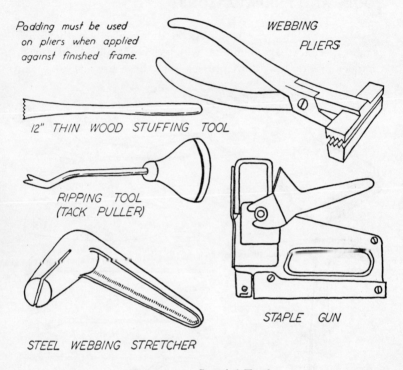

Padding must be used
on pliers when applied
against finished frame.

WEBBING
PLIERS

12" THIN WOOD STUFFING TOOL

RIPPING TOOL
(TACK PULLER)

STAPLE GUN

STEEL WEBBING STRETCHER

Figure 16—Special Tools

lowing: Shears (two sizes, ordinary sewing shears and heavy duty tailor's or bent shears); needles, assorted upholstery or sailmaker's needles including: gunny sack needle, double point-single eye heavy duty needle, and large darning needle; 2½" skewer or upholsterer's basting pin (have about 12 or 14); ice pick or eight inch stuffing regulator and a flat, smooth stuffing stick 12" long. The most necessary of these tools is the wooden webbing stretcher which can be made from a dime store ice flaker and a short piece of rubber hose or leather on the end opposite the six or seven sharp nails.

Special Tools—There are some special tools for upholstery which can be, for the most part, fabricated or purchased through some mail order house where all material for this craft is available.

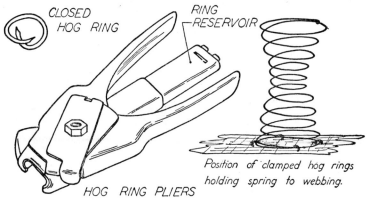

Figure 17—Hog Ring Pliers

A commercial pliers-type webbing stretcher is available and is somewhat easier to use, especially for a woman; a ripping chisel or tool, used to take out tacks and fasteners; a steel webbing band stretcher is necessary if you plan to use banding iron webbing; some sort of bolt or spring wire cutter (notching file) is necessary if you plan to use the newer sagless spring wire, which is tempered steel and would soon ruin a pair of cutting pliers of ordinary steel; a hand stapler or the hammer staple tacker (a staple makes a fine substitute for the old style carpet or upholstery tack, although it is not always as strong, it will not loosen and pull out of its hole as does the tapered tack.) If you plan to use the coil spring type of support, then a useful tool to substitute for hand sewing of the springs in place is the hog-ring pliers and open rings. This tool, shown in Fig. 17, can save time not only in sewing but in eliminating wire binding of edge wire and other units together.

Other common garden-variety tools are always useful such as a saw, regular hammer, rubber mallet, and the other general tools.

Work Surface—The work surface is an essential need unless you enjoy the prospect of refinishing the scratched wood arms and legs and various other parts which must be protected. The

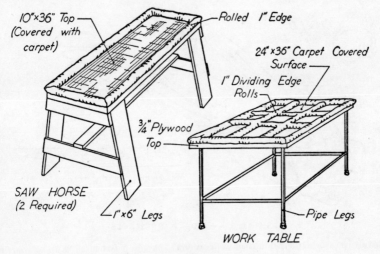

Figure 18—Work Surfaces

professional upholsterer has his own particular favorite type of work surface, a table or perhaps two wide-topped saw horses, but no matter how he has it arranged, the top surface is padded with rolled edging of some sort, as illustrated in Fig. 18.

Around the edges of both of these particular units is heavy cloth covered soft rope, about one inch in diameter. The top surface is covered with old strips of heavy carpeting. No tacks or fasteners must stick out or be in a place where the weight of the furniture will sink the padding down far enough to cause a scratch. It is assumed that you have some convenient working height, so the units should be made average height for the work you are doing. Adjustable, pre-cut, saw horse units can be purchased at the lumber yard. If you are planning to convert an old table to serve as the work surface, then, as is shown in Fig. 18, the rolled edging must be spaced about six inches apart down the center and around the edges. An extra pair of covered or top padded saw horses would facilitate the moving of the furniture from one position to the other.

I have made a special point of stressing the value of adequate lighting for your upholstering work space. You must light the work surface with as much light as you would if you were writing. Thus when well lighted there will be little chance of mistakes that will spoil the appearance of the piece. Your general work attitude is greatly affected by lighting. The project will seem easier if done under perfect working conditions. It is possible to purchase superb clamp-on spot-lamps with 75 watt reflector bulbs available at your electric company. These lamps will give all the extra light you need at the right spot and without shadows.

Materials—In upholstery and reupholstery there are materials which have changed little in hundreds of years. Perhaps the basic metals and organic structures have changed: from brass tacks to cheaper and stronger iron tacks and now automatically "shot-in" staples. There are many other examples but the important point is that these materials must be recognized and on hand when you need them. There will not be any great explanation of these different materials since in the course of the projects in this book they will either be explained or will be described by their application.

The main element of this material is the coil spring which is used in the seats, backs, and cushions. The different coils used in each application have varied forms and within those forms, several compression strengths. The Marshall Unit used in innerspring mattresses is simply coiled springs of one type sewed into a muslin bag and stitched in between, thus giving independent action to any row or section of a seat or cushion. This unit can be purchased in strips or in block units, as shown in Fig. 19. Seat springs are coils of spring wire available in different diameters ranging from #9 gauge (the largest) to #12 gauge (the smallest). They may be purchased, as all coil springs can, with open or closed end loops. (See Fig. 20.) The sizes range from 00 (5″ high) to #7 (16″ high, for hassocks, etc.). The binding and tying of these spring units will be shown in the project section concerned with this element.

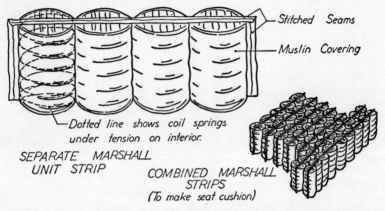

Figure 19—Marshall Units

The springs used in the backs and cushions are made of the same spring wire of a smaller gauge (12 to 15 gauge) and come in heights from four to 10 inches for backs and from

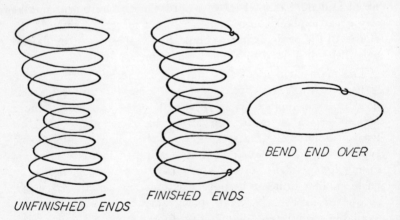

Figure 20—Coil Spring End Closures

four to eight inches for cushions. In all coil springs for uphol-stery the springs come in three compressible strengths—hard, medium and soft. All three may be the same size and height but they are wound differently. The hard spring has less steel wire in it so its coils near the center are smaller in diameter. The softer coil springs are just the converse (see Fig. 21). These coil springs may be purchased through any one of the large mail order houses.

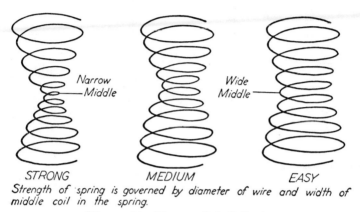

Narrow
—Middle

Wide
Middle—

STRONG   MEDIUM   EASY

Strength of spring is governed by diameter of wire and width of middle coil in the spring.

Figure 21—Types of Coil Spring

Spring wire must also be used to integrate the coil springs once the unit is constructed. This heavy wire (9 to 10 gauge) for seats must resist bending when loaded and may be bent the same as the edge wire described in the first chapter. For backs the gauge should be closer to #14. No edge wire is used in soft cushions where the springs are tied and held in place on jute (burlap). In some cases it is desirable to have a stiff edged couch or sofa cushion, then wire may be padded and used for formed work. The wire edging can be laced, tied, clamped, or clipped with hog rings (see Fig. 17). Torsion springs, shown in Fig. 6, can be used to advantage with the older type coil formation and may be added to an old unit.

Tacks are the bane of the upholsterer's existence. You may have noticed that all tacks are marked sterilized, but they don't say when—and this does not keep them from disrupting your breathing or digestion. This is by way of warning about putting tacks in your mouth. **DON'T DO IT.** These tacks are used in four major categories: webbing tacks (which have

holding cleats on the spike in order to hold the force of bulk
exerted on the webbing); gimp tacks (for hidden tacking of
decorative fringe and strips of cloth called gimp); decorative
tacks (large metal or fabric covered tacks for decorative

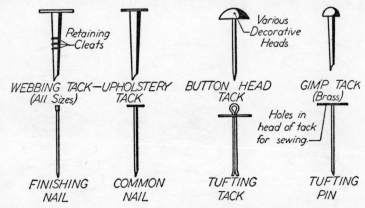

Figure 22—Types of Tacks Used in Upholstery

purposes); and finally, ordinary upholstery tacks which range
in length from ³⁄₁₆ inch to one inch in about fifteen sizes, many
of which are not necessary for good work. When the need for

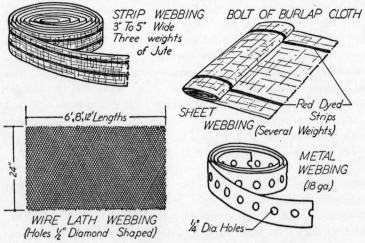

Figure 23—Different Types of Webbing

a certain tack comes along in this book it will be noted. (See Fig. 22.)

The cloth used in upholstery work under the finished exterior runs from light weight burlap to heavy muslin. Burlap comes in several weights, though 10-ounce can be used with surety throughout the complete job of covering coil springs, padding, and sagless springs. Webbing (types of which are shown in Fig. 23) can be obtained in the same material and can also be purchased in light weights with little difference in cost and thus is better to use. The widths are 3, 3½, and 4"; there is little need to have more than the 3½" width unless you are going into business. Muslin is obtained in either bleached or unbleached form and it makes no difference which is used. Muslin forms easily over contoured stuffing and is easily tacked or stapled. Unvarnished cambric is used as a covering on the bottom of the webbing so as to obscure its burlap ugliness from low glances. Once tacked in place it can be sized or soaked with starch to make it dustproof, but it tends to tear rather easily unless you have installed steel strap webbing which must be tensioned with the webbing stretcher described in Fig. 16. Burlap webbing retains its shape only if not sat upon. After a time it will break or give way as the tacks slip out. The exterior material should always be of the very best grade since you will not be anxious to recover this particular piece again soon. It is a wise investment to cut a pattern from heavy muslin or canvas before cutting the Swiss brocade or whatever. (This will be explained further). In all upholstery or reupholstery work, padding is a constant source of vermin, rot and lumps. If the correct material is chosen and correctly applied, then no further trouble is encountered. The rubber covered fibers and padding are a safe bet, but some do not prefer this material and would rather stay with horse hair and swamp moss. Egyptian and southern cotton, illustrated in Fig. 24, have been used for many sections of the upholsterer's job; the filling of cushions, padding, and "insulating" felting (used to keep the sub- or under-stuffing from poking through, or to cover the tied springs, this has generally been superseded by foam rubber padding except in very cheap furniture). Since the fibers of cotton tend to matt down it should not be used for filler except where this effect will not be noticed or for places which bear no great amount of weight such as in arms, wings, channels or corner fillers in overstuffed pieces. When used correctly over all underpadding and stuffing, including spring insulation it tends to quiet the scratching or compressing noise. The very best natural stuffing or filler is long strand

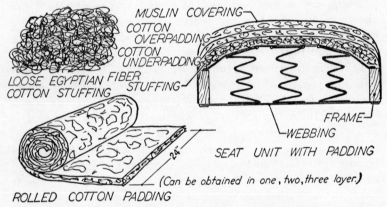

Figure 24—Cotton Padding and Stuffing

curly horse and cow hair (not mixed with hog hair—an undesirable short bristle). This material is subject to moths and vermin and should be treated with some form of modern permanent repellent powder. Other stuffing materials include kapok, which resembles milkweed down; Spanish moss, sisal and coco fibers, wood excelsior (not at all satisfactory and only used in the worst grade of furniture), and down (including processed feathers) used in pillows and soft stuffing. It will never matt down, or lump together, can be washed and dried in the sack, but is monstrously hard to work with. I would recommend using foam rubber and its companion materials, the rubber and plastic coated fibers, instead. Many of the professionals will stick to the other materials but their craftsmanship makes the difference between workability and not. Do not conclude that furniture constructed and upholstered with these materials of old is no longer any good. This is, of course, not true. The main difference is that for the amateur the new materials are easier to use.

Trim and gimp are extremely important to the finished job. The trim includes such things as ready-rolled edges, formed matting, cushions ready for covering, and tacking strips for straight blind tacking of the top covering. The latter is made of heavy cardboard and comes in rolls much as ticker tape, about ½ inch in width. Gimp is a binding material used on

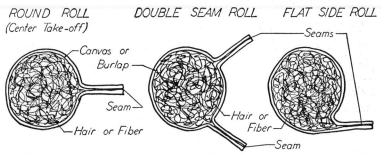

A new paper covered edge roll in these shapes is obtainable and has proven most successful in lasting quality over burlap.

Figure 25—Types of Rolled Edging

the exterior of the unit either for decoration or for covering unsightly upholstery tacks. It is made of a variety of materials and can be easily improvised or purchased at any dry goods store. Sometimes it is stiffened with steel wire so as to form around sharp curves. The modern trend is toward blind tacking and no gimp—difficult to effect, but worthwhile in its simplicity.

Rolled edging comes ready made in several diameters. It is used where you desire to have a sharp but soft edge or curve (see Fig. 25). The different diameters range from ½″ to 1½″ and can be obtained with a variety of stuffing. When edge wire is used in a place where it cannot be protected by later padding, then an edge roll can be sewn or laced to it before the exterior is applied. Care must be taken that these ready rolled strips are securely tacked or sewn in place. Often in cheap upholstery the under padding will slip, causing the loosely attached rolled edge to go out of place.

The variety of other materials used in upholstery and reupholstery is left up to the craftsman, who may desire a special type of covering for strength, or decoration. One of the most widely used under-materials which exhibits a great deal of strength and durability is ticking, the striped material so often seen on down pillows. It comes in standard widths and can be obtained in several weights. It is a good material for practice in covering your final job. This practice cover can be taken off or left on as you choose prior to the application of the final cover.

Twine is the last of the important materials but one that must be stressed in its quality. No matter how good your upholstery job is, the spring or tying twine is its weakest link. There are several types of twine and many brand names. Buy twine made for this purpose. Lacing twine is made from flax and is used to tie together heavy elements, where ordinary thread will not hold. It can be purchased in strengths from three-ounce to 12-ounce and is sometimes waxed. Tying and spring twines are made from jute, as is burlap, and may be purchased in pound size rolls.

Chapter 3

FRAME CONSTRUCTION AND RECONSTRUCTION

It is not the intention of this book to go into the building of furniture but rather the problems of covering it for comfort and decoration. However, it is often necessary to reinforce the frame to be recovered, or a new frame on which you wish to use sagless springs or other new material needing stronger frames. We will cover the problems of correcting weakened frames and adding new bracing members.

Gluing

There are many "old wives' tales" about the art of gluing; many of them are true. The most recent glues tend to refute the old masters to an extent. You must consider what glue is asked to do in most cases. The average craftsman asks glue to perform what nature did not do, that is, grow a complete chair or cabinet frame. Let's forget this fallacy and proceed to what the proper use of glue should be. The cardinal rules of proper gluing are these: First, the unit must be well fit in the cutting of its separate pieces. Second, the unit must be planned so that the different members (legs, arms, backs and others) do not get the chance to act as levers against each other to break whatever glue joints are used. This is to say the structure must be sound. Glue by itself is not sufficient to fasten two pieces of material together; there must be sufficient mechanical strength in the joint effected by the two pieces.

In the process of regluing, the same rules must be observed with the addition of the very important fact of making sure the old glue has been thoroughly removed. Fig. 26 shows places where joints most often need repair. If sections of wood have broken away, these must be replaced in order to assure a tight joint.

In the past it was assumed that extreme clamping pressure was necessary to make a good glue joint. This may have been

true with the older animal and fish glues but as the new polyvinyl glues appeared it was found that too much clamping
pressure would force the bonding glue out of the joint. The
phenolic resin glues which are set under pressure and heat are
the best type of furniture glues, but usually they are used
only in the factory. In new construction, the new types of

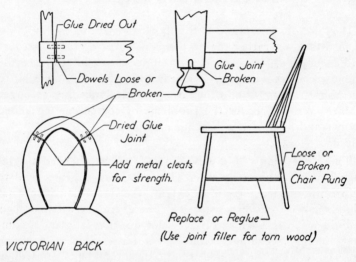

Figure 26—Furniture Joints Most Often in Need of Repair

polyvinyl and catalyst resin glues are the best. In regluing
where animal glues were used it is wise to reglue with the
newer types of animal glue. It is no longer necessary to heat
the glue flakes in the glue pot as this glue can now be obtained
in liquid form. With the animal glues, heavier pressure is
used, thus the need arises for metal or wooden clamps. With
the newer glue sufficient pressure can be obtained by using
clothesline (padded where it goes around the furniture) and
a twisting stick, as shown in Fig. 27. Sufficient time should be
allowed for all glue to set properly and the best advice is to
follow closely the directions on the glue container.

Metal Fasteners

In all furniture construction there occur places where the
frame must be braced in addition to the regular joint between

the two members. In most furniture these braces or blocks are made of wood, drilled for screws and fastened with glue and

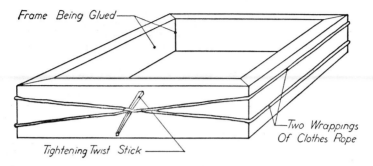

Figure 27—Clothesline Clamp

the screws to either side of the corner (see Fig. 28). Often in repair work on furniture it is necessary to re-install these cleats, blocks or braces and if the part is missing, metal angle fasteners or braces are a perfect substitute, and can be

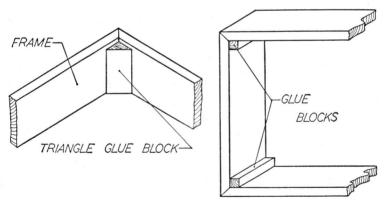

Figure 28—Bracing Cleats and Glue Blocks

obtained in many sizes and shapes. If the standard shapes do not conform to the angle of the piece then these braces can be bent in a machinist's vice until they fit. Their application without glue is made simply by several screws of the proper length.

The use of wood screws has almost entirely taken the place of cut nails and pegs, though pegs are still used in most furniture joints. The choice of the correct length and size of screw is most important. When a wood screw is used to hold two objects together, the joining is accomplished by the screw holding one piece to the other by its threaded section biting

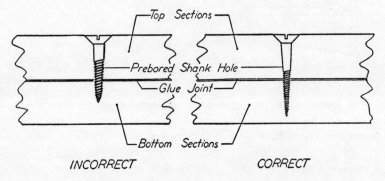

INCORRECT   CORRECT

Figure 29—Wood Screw Application

into the bottom piece and the shank and the head of the screw simply fiitting snugly through the top piece with no threads catching in it (see Fig. 29). In choosing the right screw, the thickness of the wood in which the shank will rest and the screw will bite must be considered. There must be few threads remaining in the top piece, if any, and the screw point should be at least ⅛ inch from the surface (see Fig. 29) so that sanding or finishing will not uncover the metal. In sizing screws, the smaller the size number the smaller the diameter of the screws. They are made from several types of metal (brass, iron, stainless steel) and can be obtained in lengths from ¼ inch to six inches. The most general type of head used in upholstery is the flat head, though others (round, oval, pan head) will do.

Corrugated wood fasteners are available in several sizes as are Scotch fasteners, both shown in Fig. 30. These units are used to join two pieces of wood which have been glued but are impossible to brace, because of inaccessibility, in any other way. They are pounded into the two pieces in question and tend to draw them together. Flat metal screw plates can also be used for this same purpose.

Finish

In all upholstery work it is advisable to do all the finishing and refinishing of the exposed parts of the frame when the covering has been removed, or before any padding or covering

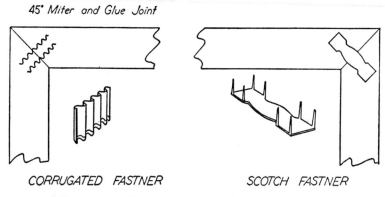

Figure 30—Corrugated and Scotch Fasteners

has been applied. The finish of the wood and metal parts is a matter of personal choice. For advice on the correct process see Drake's Book on Wood Finishing.

Reforming or Restyling

Many times it is as easy to restyle or reform the old frame as it is to reupholster the old style frame. Fig. 31 shows how simple restyling can enhance the appearance of a furniture piece. The old fashioned arms may be squared off with the addition of wooden members. The ornate wood backs may be cut off or covered with a squaring piece of wood. Wings may be added to the occasional chair just as the old ones may be removed. Legs may be cut off to make the seating height lower, arms may be lengthened or removed (unless they form a bracing member for the frame, as they often do). The open arm of a chair or love seat may be closed in and padded for upholstery, all that is necessary for padding and upholstering a section of any piece of furniture is forming the under frame of the section in the general shape of what you want in the final piece. The upholstery material will give it full form in its finished style.

Restyling Cushions and Separate Parts of any Piece

The older pieces of furniture had unshaped and unsupported (springless) cushions. With a unit such as a sofa, the three cushions can be transformed into the more modern double

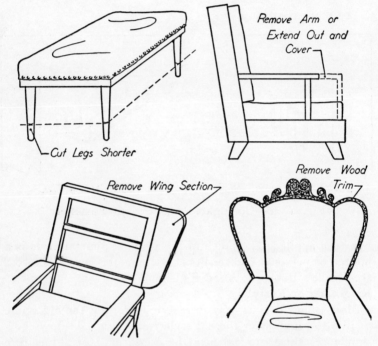

Figure 31—Suggested Areas for Restyling

cushions or the long single foam rubber mat cushion. The incorporation of the already covered and tied Marshall units is a relatively easy substitute for the stuffed cushion. Soft extra cushions can be filled with down, or made from old bed pillows.

The backs of the unit may be left unpadded and an extra cushion made in substantial form (foam rubber or Marshall units) thus giving the old piece a new look. While in the process of restyling it is best to consider the necessity of extra bracing in the various sections of the piece of furniture, if you are going to use the sagless spring, as has been mentioned previously. The following discussion will show where the most tension will occur in any frame.

Long Seats—The sagless springs are stretched from the front to back rail and on the top of these two rails. If the

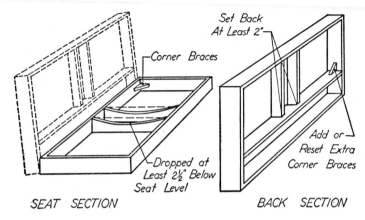

SEAT SECTION   BACK SECTION

Figure 32—Sagless Spring Frame Supports for Long Seats
Figure 33—Sagless Spring Frame Supports for Long Backs

frame is not strong enough, the frame will tend to bow in and if the dowelling or joint at either end of the frame rails is not secure, the rails will twist vertically in time. If the rails are five feet or under, then one strong cross support from front to back will suffice, if longer than five feet two supports are necessary (see Figs. 32 and 33).

Backs—The same precautions should be taken in the springing of backs, since the springs extend from top to bottom rail. The supports need not be so strong as in the case of the seats since the back sagless springs are usually of less tension.

Arms—No extra bracing is necessary other than an additional member onto which will be fastened one end of the sagless springs.

Fastening Members—All fastening members for the ends or clips of the sagless springs should be at least 1″ thick. Often it is necessary to bring up the level of the rails by adding an

extra fastening strip. This strip should be glued and fastened
in place with screws. The reason for additional height is not
alone for leveling to take the place of old padding, but it also
gives extra fastening strength.

Smaller Seats—In the case of smaller seats where the
tension of the springs are not sufficient to warp the frame, it
is only necessary to check the corner braces on the inside of
the seat for strength and to be sure that they are at least one
inch below the level of the seat frame. If these blocks or
braces must be changed there are two alternatives: either
knock them out, or build up the seat edge around the frame.
It is not always wise to remove them from a securely glued
frame. In older furniture these blocks are often loose anyway.

Preparation for Webbing—In new frames there are no
necessary changes which have to be made in order to use
webbing support on both the top and bottom of the furniture
in question. In reupholstery the only problem which will arise
is the tacking strip which, during the course of years and
many reupholstery jobs, has become pitted and split with
the application of many tacks. If this is the case, then it is
advisable wherever possible to apply (with glue and wood
screws) a tacking strip. These strips can vary in thickness
from $\frac{1}{2}''$ to $1''$ and should run completely the length of the
tacking rail in question and around all other rails to level the
tacking surface. It is not advisable to try to fill the cracks and
holes with filler since it becomes harder than the surrounding
wood, and the tacks will tend to force off their mark rather
than enter the hardened filler. Cleated webbing tacks are
advised since the greatest force is exerted on the webbing,
especially that on the bottom of the frame.

Steel Strap Webbing—No special preparation other than
that mentioned previously is necessary to support steel webbing. The special tool used in the pulling of steel webbing
must not be used with too much strength. This needless practice could warp the frame. In the application of steel webbing
there is no necessity to lace the strapping since it scarcely
gives under load and will not shift. The strapping can be
located on $2''$ centers for complete spring positioning. Thus
the springs can be tied securely no matter where they happen

to fall. The springs, either Marshall units or separate springs can be laced with fine wire or string. Hog rings, previously illustrated in Fig. 17, can be used to clamp these securely in place. If steel webbing is to be used on a piece of furniture which will be subject to moisture, it is best to coat the webbing with either red-lead or Rustoeleum paint. In the ordinary application this is not necessary.

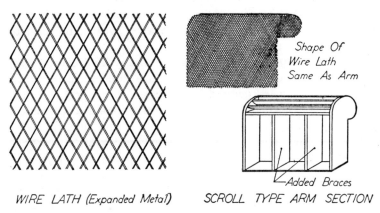

WIRE LATH (Expanded Metal)   SCROLL TYPE ARM SECTION

Figure 34 *(left)*—**Wire Lath**
Figure 35 *(right)*—**Wire Lath Applied Over Curved Section**

One-inch steel webbing may be added over existing cloth webbing on 4″ centers, or may be used as the only webbing. It is especially advisable if the person to generally occupy the chair is over-weight. If excessive weight is contemplated the steel strapping could be fastened in place with screws rather than 3-penny coated nails or roofing tacks. One special note of caution: Steel webbing is only recommended for application to the bottom supporting webbing and not to either side or top webbing, since it is difficult to cover up the existence of such narrow and hard stripping.

Wire lath, which has been used for many years in the plastering trade, has recently become a material for use in upholstery done at home. This material, shown in Fig. 34, is light and strong and has resiliency enough to be a good bottoming webbing material. It can be tacked, laced and formed. There have been many cases where it has been used to advantage in forming other parts of the piece being either upholstered or reupholstered. Wire lath can be easily cut with tin shears. Care must be taken to either fold over the edges or to pound them into the wood frame. Since it is possible to tack this metal in many places there is no necessity to use nails or screws. A webbing tack (cleated) placed every inch will give all the support necessary. When the final unit is covered it is suggested that a somewhat heavier material than cambric, such as muslin or some dark dyed material of a heavier weave, be used to cover the bottom.

Unusual Shaped Chairs—Webbing of any kind can be used on curved surfaces but it is sometimes difficult to form the strips on the curved edging. If this is a difficult problem then the use of steel webbing or steel lath can simplify the problem (see Fig. 35). By the use of a rubber mallet or a wooden sledge mallet, the steel lath can be rounded or bowed into the desired shape. Where extreme strength is necessary two layers of steel lath can be used. It is also possible to back this material up with sagless springs. You will find that it gives a very smooth surface and the stuffing or padding can be easily sewn to it because of its open weave effect. If it is necessary to make unusual shapes for this material it can be heated over a gas burner and allowed to cool without dipping it in water (quenching), thus upon cooling it is soft and pliable and able to be formed. After you have fitted the piece to the place you desire, it must be reheated to the same dull red glow and then dipped in water (quenched), thus returning it to its same spring hardness. It will only serve to add problems to your work if you do not regard the sharp cut ends which are not only a danger to the hand but to snagging the material used in further covering of the furniture.

Chapter 4

PLANNING—MATERIALS AND PROCEDURE

As has been done in many other books on this same subject I will try to cover all of the material that is necessary to the actual upholstery or reupholstery of any particular piece of furniture. However, since the design of every piece is somewhat different and your taste is different than that of the author who chooses certain pieces for any book, I am going to try to cover all pieces in one example. That is, there will be two examples: one a chair, and one a sofa. The chair will have all the various styles of every chair and the sofa can be a love seat just 36″ wide or a sofa eight feet long. It is up to you to adjust the examples to your exact measurements. In the case of the chair, I will show it with one type of arm on one side and another type on the other. I will show how to make the seat practical in several different ways, the back in several styles. Were you to try to put this particular chair together it would be a hodge-podge of grotesqueness, but all in all it will be a better device to show the beginner just what he can do with the art of upholstery (or reupholstery) with limited knowledge. The same will apply to the love seat or the long sofa. If there are questions that seem as though they have not been answered, then leaf through the various explanations again and the answer will be found. Thus we will cut down the amount of reading and remembering that you will have to do for any one job.

I must caution you again that these are not projects in the normal sense of the usual repetitious do-it-yourself book, but these projects each include one of the problems that will be encountered in the various types of furniture for upholstery that fall under the class: Chair or Sofa. **Do not try to build one of these units—it will cause you no end of trouble.** I am sure no one will try the impossible. The explanations will

45

progress from those which came before. If there is any question, then go back to earlier explanations and descriptions.

General Measurements

If the job or project with which you are involved is one of reupholstery, then the simplest manner of obtaining the correct measurements is to strip the old covering off down to the muslin covering and then lay out the old covering according to the warp or woof (common threads running one way) of the cloth. This will give you a perfect idea of how much cloth will be involved in the recovering of the unit. If there is a great deal of restyling, then the final measurement must be reckoned with. Do not skimp on the amount of cloth or material used; there is no economy in saving the cost of a yard of material, and trying to make it do by stretching tighter than the cloth should be stretched or by tacking too close to the edge of the cloth. Every element in any upholstery project should be planned as though it were to be used in a public movie house and subjected to the most severe wear and abuse.

If the piece of furniture is to be stripped to the frame, then do not go halfway; check all the joints. Any in question should be reglued or strengthened. Never use old stuffing or padding. Never under any circumstance use old cloth or burlap webbing, since age causes it to dry out and lose strength. Springs, wire and other metal parts do not lose their strength and may be used over again. However, if the piece is very old, then the wire and springs are apt to be of a poor spring steel temper and should be replaced with modern material. Tying string or cord never can be used more than once and should be of extremely good quality when it is chosen the first time. As has been explained before the whole project can be a waste with poor material. **Planning is important.**

Before we begin, let's take a look at the general types of chairs and sofas, examples of which are illustrated in Fig. 36. All of these can be classed according to the types of backs and the arm and wings which are incorporated into their design. The wing chair is little different than the English Deep Sofa Seat, and the ordinary modern couch is little different than the Lawson chair or the conventional "man of the house" chair. Length seems to be the greatest difference. Whether a chair or sofa has wings or not the basic frame is little different. The following are the general types of edges, backs, tops, fronts, cushioned seats, legs, and gimp or trim. These types will be explained further as the text goes on, but the illustrations will show what is to be expected in the final job as far as outward shape and design is concerned.

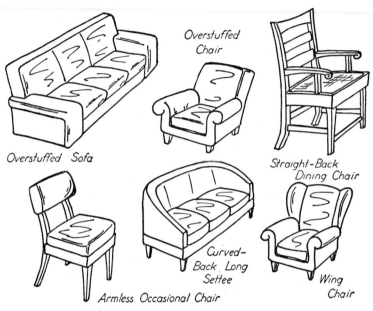

Figure 36—Some General Types of Furniture

The type of spring material to be used will be covered for each case where different materials can be used or substituted. In cases where it is most advisable to use one type or the other there will be but slight mention, if any, of other alternatives. The first choice and the wisest, of course, will be noted or exampled first. If there is any question then a review of the first explanations will, I am sure, clarify the problem. Mistakes which are noticed in time are important to correct, but those which come to light at a stage too far advanced to rectify are better forgotten unless they are too evident. Many times these errors are not noticeable to anyone other than the craftsman. On smaller jobs these mistakes show up to a greater disadvantage than on a bigger project. Perfection comes to the craftsman only by his practice of any craft, and not with the first job.

Starting to Reupholster

Since this is the element with which most people are concerned, we will treat it first.

The first step in any job of this type is to remove the old covering; this is of great importance since its size governs the amount of material you will use to recover the same piece. The following steps are of great importance:

1st—Remove all gimp or trim and save for measurement.

2nd—Remove all upholstery tacks which hold the covering material only. With this step remove all covered arm fronts and save them as templets if you intend to re-install these pieces on the recovered unit.

3rd—Now that the unit of furniture is down to the muslin covering and nothing more is needed to repair the unit, then lay out the pieces of fabric that made up the old covering and make sure that the warp and woof (the grain of the fabric) is correct. Bear in mind that most material is measured by the yard in length and is usually fifty-four inches wide. Lay out the pieces so that they correspond to this set of dimensions. If your material is narrower, as are some of the better materials, it is wise to know just what the correct width is. Allow at least one yard for coverage as there are many cases where the material needs extra selvege (edge) to be applied. When laying out and cutting these pieces be sure to leave 2½ to 3 inches between each section. Fig. 37 shows a typical material layout for recovering a chair. In the case of the plan that includes restyling of the piece in question, measurement of the old fabric will only be a general guide. If your restyling takes the form of removal then the amount of external cloth will be less, and conversely if the frame has added dimensions.

4th—The recovering process is not involved if there is no repadding, stuffing or webbing to do. There are many people who feel that to recover a piece of furniture with upholstery material is easier than making a slip cover. This is true in most cases where there is involved a muslin undercovering.

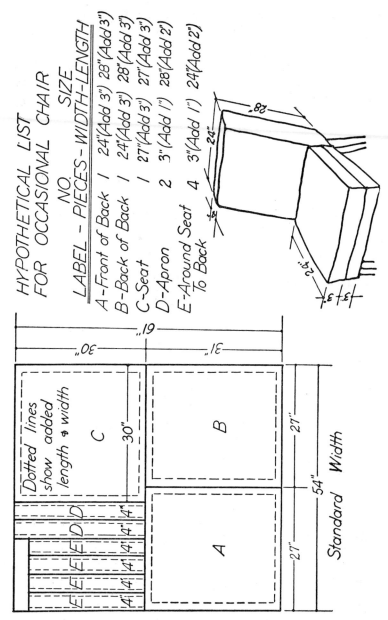

HYPOTHETICAL LIST
FOR OCCASIONAL CHAIR

LABEL - PIECES - WIDTH-LENGTH	NO.	SIZE
A - Front of Back	1	24"(Add 3") 28"(Add 3")
B - Back of Back	1	24"(Add 3") 28"(Add 3")
C - Seat	1	27"(Add 3") 27"(Add 3")
D - Apron	2	3"(Add 1") 28"(Add 2")
E - Around Seat To Back	4	3"(Add 1") 24"(Add 2")

Figure 37—Layout of Material for Chair Covering

If once you have stripped the piece and found that there is no general undercovering then it is best to practice your work with the application of an undercovering of muslin. It is not a very expensive addition to your project but will result in a much better finished project in the long run. Fig. 38 shows the undercovering applied and the necessary points of tacking.

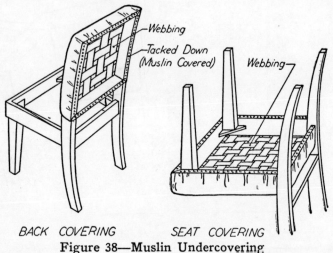

BACK COVERING   SEAT COVERING

Figure 38—Muslin Undercovering

If there is to be a fixed cushion where there was not one before or vice versa, then further on in this text the explanation and directions will be given. Otherwise the chair is to be finished as it was with the old covering. The fixed cushion is an added part and not involved with the primary work. If the cushion is to be used as is, it may be either recovered or have a foam rubber base, or Marshall units (springs) may be added. This process will be discussed in the chapter dealing with cushions. Other question on particular parts of each unit will be answered as we go along.

5th—The final tacking and stretching of material will be discussed in one of the last chapters in this book since it is essentially the same for all types of furniture. If your project does not involve anything but simple recovering, then this chapter will give you the necessary information to complete it.

6th—Plastic or imitation leather covering is often desired

because of its superior wearing qualities. There are several vinyl plastics which can scarcely be distinguished from real leather. While the use of real leather gives a beautiful appearance it is wise to let the expert do the job. Leather is considered by many as the most difficult of all coverings to work with, and plastic is considered as perhaps the easiest due to its easy conformity to the structure of the furniture. There are, however, certain very important factors to consider before you can proceed as you would with cloth.

1. Not all sheet plastic is advised for use in upholstering. Seek more specific information from individual manufacturers.

2. Most plastics will dissolve easily with solvents used in cleaning or furniture polish. Some wax solvents will destroy certain plastics.

3. Most solid plastics cannot be painted or dyed; those in the category of imitation leather (painted cloth) can, however, be painted with non-lacquer type paints.

4. When a hole or sharp corner is cut, care must be taken not to leave a jagged edge or scissors' nicks in its circumference. A half-inch smooth corner should be cut with the aid of a leather punch or ground-off pipe, as shown in Fig. 39. Before either the corner is cut or a hole is punched, it is very important to back up the plastic with either Mystic tape or plain wide adhesive tape. On edges where a considerable number of tacks will be applied, a strip of backing will keep the plastic from tearing under force. When tacking plastic, do not pound the head of the tack too firmly into the surface of the plastic. Large headed tacks are best.

5. Repairing plastic covering can be done in several ways. If the tear or burned hole is accessible from both sides then sewing a patch in place will afford a serviceable mend. However, if the spot to be repaired must be concealed as well as possible then the following procedure is to be followed, remembering that any transparent glue will dissolve the surface of the plastic wherever it touches it. Any solvent which might be used to clean off the surplus glue will ruin the surface. The glue must be of the colloidal type (model makers glue) and not the animal or polyvinyl type.

The glue must be used sparingly, to act as a solvent only to weld together the torn edges. Follow these steps:

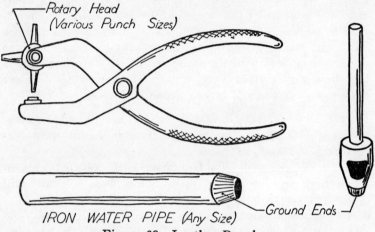

IRON WATER PIPE (Any Size)
Figure 39—Leather Punches

a. If the hole is torn rather than melted or dissolved (fingernail polish, etc.), a patch can be cut from plastic of similar color and inserted without glue through the rent or tear and centered under the hole. At least a one-inch border is needed around the hole. If the tear is not large enough (about one inch long) to insert the reinforcement piece then enlarge the hole with a pair of scissors.

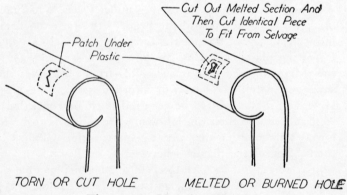

TORN OR CUT HOLE   MELTED OR BURNED HOLE
Figure 40—Mending Plastic

b. If the hole has been caused by a hot object or solvent and has a ragged appearance, then it is necessary to pare away some of the rough edges, making the hole larger (see Fig. 40). Now follow preceding instructions given under "a" and then cut to size a piece of plastic the same size as the enlarged hole. Extra pieces of plastic covering may be obtained from tacking edges under the piece being repaired.

c. In both cases of repair shown in Fig. 40, use a small cotton or cloth-covered matchstick and insert a small amount of thin glue between the patch and the top covering. Do not overglue. Then gently apply a very small amount of glue to the edges of the tear or insert patch, using masking tape to hold the mend together till dry (24 hours).

d. After the patch has dried with the edges welded together with a small amount of glue, an inspection will show any openings which have not been mended. A tooth pick and a small amount of glue will mend these with the use of masking tape to pull them together. Care must be exercised not to allow the drops of glue that sometimes string off the end of the tube to fall on the plastic covering, since they immediately dissolve the plastic and cannot be removed.

e. When the patch is complete, small rough spots can be very gently scraped or sanded smooth if patient effort is applied. After the process of smoothing is complete a small amount of good table wax (solid type) will gloss over the finish of the patch.

f. The repair of painted cloth (leatherette) can be done in the same manner or by sewing. It is possible to repaint the mended patch with artists oils so that the mend is unobtrusive.

g. Sewing involved in any patch work must be done with a curved upholsterer's needle and appropriate thread. The stitches in plastic must be far enough apart so that they do not form a line of holes along which the material will tear. Leatherette can be sewn closer to the tear and at any interval which seems suitable, because of its bonding coat of paint. This painted cloth is not advised for covering material since the paint tends to peal after exposure to flexing and moisture. General upholstery sewing (machine sewing) will be discussed later in the book.

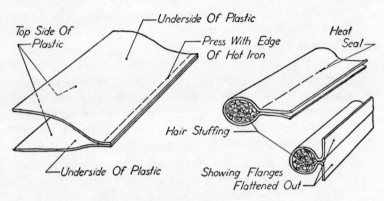

Figure 41—Heat-Sealing Plastic

h. Thickness is of great importance when choosing the correct plastic for different applications. The seat, arms and exposed areas should be covered with a heavy grade and the backs and sides with a lighter grade. Never use a weight less than .012" of any plastic. The heavier the better in plastic covering, providing it can be applied when it is above 80° F. If the plastic is cold there is a tendency to resist conforming over odd shapes and contours. The plastic may be warmed without harm by wrapping it around the hot water heater or tank, providing it does not hit any parts of the heater which are hot enough to melt it. It is wise to cut the pieces accord- to the pattern and then wrap them around the heater. In this manner there is little chance of stretching the material before it is cut to size.

i. In some of the newer types of plastic covering the material may be heat-sealed along the seams of new coverings. The thick plastic sheet is cut to the size necessary to cover the piece of furniture or unit. One inch extra is left to form an inside seam which can be heat-sealed with an ordinary flatiron at low temperature (see Fig. 41). Once the two pieces are heat-sealed there is no way to separate them. Extreme care must be taken to insure the correct fit of the plastic to the object being covered.

This method is especially useful in forming covered padding rolls and shapes, since the sealed edge can be hidden under other covering.

In the past years there have appeared on the market several types of cloth woven from metals (aluminum, stainless steel) and glass fibers. These cloths are extremely difficult to handle and it is advised that if you plan to use any of these long-wearing materials you write to the company who weaves them. Do not try to apply them in the same fashion as plastic or ordinary upholstery cloth.

Chapter 5

FURNITURE UNITS

Seats

There are only a few definite classifications of seats which are commonly found in household furniture. These all have experienced the variations of the craftsman through the years. All these types to be mentioned are shown in Fig. 42.

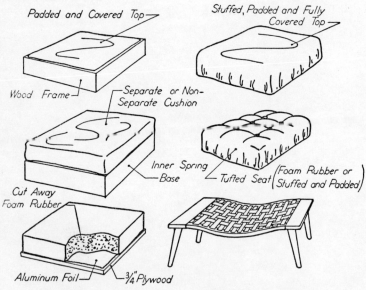

Figure 42—Some Standard Types of Seats

The two major divisions for overstuffed pieces are those with separate cushions and those without. Each may not appear much different from the other, but each has its advantages.

Separate cushions, reversible and non-reversible, include those shaped with the "T" front and those which are square.

These cushions, as has been mentioned before, are stuffed and filled in various manners. Edges are of a personal preference and may be styled by the method of stuffing and springing any set of cushions. Each of the major types will be explained.

The placement of the seat separation is much a matter of piece design and preference. In some cases the split cushion is desirable over the older three-segment seat or the modern single unit. Plans must be made prior to the covering of the piece for tacking and bracing strips must be added in some cases. Tufting, and lining (segmenting, in curved backs or long seats) has been a preference in more classic decors.

The "in place" cushion must also be planned for since it is part of the construction in the upholstery or reupholstery of the unit. It has its advantages in that it is easier to install, spring and pad, yet the disadvantages of wearing out more rapidly come to the front. The application of the unit must be considered. Where there are active children, fixed cushions are not advised. Sponge or foam rubber would be most suitable since any type of spring unit will eventually wear through or break apart.

Single Chair or Small Seats—In the application of a covering or padding on a small seat such as a dining room chair or an occasional chair, it is wise to remember that the smaller the unit the greater the wearing tension. Square frame seats can be filled in with different types of webbing, burlap, plywood for foam rubber, or even the legs of the chair can be cut and the seat built up for spring padding of either type (sagless, or coil). Unless the chair seat is of a special type such as non-padded with heavy nap wool cloth covering, or leather slung, the webbing should go on the top of the frame so as to eliminate the extra padding that the thickness of the frame would take. If it is your intention to use sagless spring units in the small seat area then special care must be given to the condition of the frame and its solidity.

Occasional Chair or Curved Bench Seats—It is practically impossible to use any other type seat supports than solid curved wood or standard jute (burlap) webbing, when the seat must curve down in the Roman bench style (Fig. 42). The webbing must be slung with a small amount of sag in order to form a comfortable seat. The additional padding will take this primary shape. The occasional chair which involves no arms or back upholstery can be easily recovered or completely reupholstered. Since these chairs are usually spring "loaded" the webbing should be replaced and must be applied to the bottom of the frame. If foam rubber is desired then the webbing may be applied to the top over a solid piece of plywood ½" thick with air holes drilled 6" on center, set into the frame.

Standard Benches (Piano and Other)—The usual piano bench is simply a padded flat board with a double cover (muslin first), the edges of which are stretched by hand down over the edges of the board and tacked into the underneath side, making a neat folded edge.

Outdoor and Porch Furniture—The problem of moisture and weather gives the amateur upholsterer a fair-sized obstacle. Most kinds of materials can be used outside providing the coverings are moisture and rain proof. Steel springs soon rust through the upholstery or will rust on the bottom webbing and, in turn, cause it to rot and break. The spring units can be painted with rustproof paint. Ordinary paint will not do since it will come off with moisture. Also, if the spring is flexed a great deal in use the paint will peel. If any type of padding is to be used, it is suggested that rubber or plastic coated hair or fibers (coco, hemp, etc.) be installed. Foam rubber is good only if it is sealed by either a "Pliofilm" bag or some other waterproof plastic (a large sheet of "Saran Wrap" is the perfect covering in all foam rubber applications). Metal webbing, either strap or plasterer's expanded wire lath, can be used, but must also be painted. Stainless steel springs and strapping can be purchased at about five times the cost of ordinary material. The final covering should be some form of plastic coated cloth or solid plastic which can be sealed in the seams with gasket cement (no colloidal or model cement), applied from the under side before the spring units or cushions are stuffed.

Solid Outdoor Seats (Rubber Padded)—Before the foam rubber is applied to the top solid board, air holes should be drilled through the board's surface 6" on center, and the plywood (exterior grade) should be sealed and painted. Then a sheet of heavy grade aluminum foil should be glued on with either gasket cement or the same paint used to seal the board. The aluminum foil may have to be overlapped unless you are using freezer width. This overlap (2″) should be sealed also, then the foam rubber can be applied, either tacked or glued in place.

Automobile Seats—It is not usually economical or wise to dismantle the spring construction of automobile seats, but they can be more easily recovered with cloth than they can be slipcovered (and at not much difference in cost). The spring steel and steel webbing used in automobile seats and backs are of an extremely heavy grade due to the force applied to them when hitting road bumps and to the practice of more than one person sitting on the seat at a time. The upholstery used in most modern cars is made of the best wool and woven with large size yarn on a close loom. If through some accident to the seat you need to recover it, you will find that a set of good seat covers will run higher than the cost of the cloth used by the manufacturer. And the latter is readily obtainable from his parts division. It is not necessary to buy a completely new seat. The sewing must be done on a machine much like that used in making a suit of clothes with heavy thread (#40 or #60 cotton or nylon). The general plan of all seats is the same with the exception of the types of tufting. If care is taken in the removal of the old material, the method of application can be written down and followed precisely in recovering. Since the frame of the car seat is made of channel iron or extruded tern plate (body steel of a heavier grade), the upholstery is held in place by expanding tacks (split shafts which spread naturally) which are poked through holes pre-drilled in this metal. Other parts are wired or clipped in place by "hog" rings. Extremely tight fits are vital in all car upholstery.

Backs

There is not much difference in the application of upholstery to the backs of different pieces of furniture. In most cases the chief problems come in configuration. The straight spring loaded or foam rubber back is little different than its counterpart in the seat. All the elements of the back which include the webbing (usually just cloth webbing), the springs, forming

and edge wire are of somewhat lesser strength than those of
the seat. However, this need not be since often it is harder to
find the two types of springs and a thinner jute webbing and
the difference in cost is negligible. The various shapes of backs
are shown in Fig. 43.

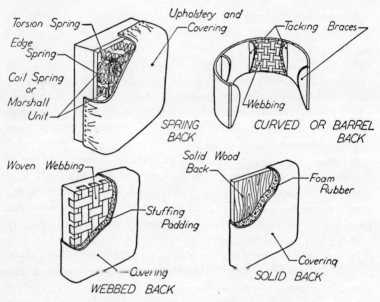

Figure 43—Some Standard Types of Backs

Spring-Loaded Backs—Where the back on a piece of furniture is to be equipped with springs of either the open coil or
Marshall Unit type, the webbing must be placed on the back
of the frame with the ends of either the vertical webbing strips
or horizontal webbing strips tacked on the inside of the frame
for more support. If the sagless spring is to be used, then the
webbing can be applied to the back simply as a base to hold
the final covering material smooth and prevent indents from
being caused in its surface. Where coil springs are used,
they are to be first covered with an "Insulator," shown in Fig.
10, and then foam rubber. The retaining webbing need not be
tensioned quite so tight, as the "insulator" tends to distribute
the force against the webbing over a wider area.

Curved Backs—The curved back, as on a Barrel Chair, etc., involves no great problems for the amateur unless this back is a spring unit, then the job will involve considerable attention as to how the former covering was applied. In some cases, replacing one piece of webbing at a time proves to be the better method and does not involve too much work at one time. The simple padded curved back may involve only webbing applied vertically on the face of the back frame, but usually, if it is possible to weave in and out, several strips of webbing are woven horizontally so that they are loose and will conform to the curve of the back. When not tensioned, this horizontal webbing is simply held in place by the tensioned vertical strips. Horizontal strips are not advised where they must be longer than 30″ between tacking points.

Straight Padded Backs—These backs can be webbed both vertically and horizontally with the webbing tacked in the front of the frame where it can be easily covered with any form of padding. In these cases, where the back of the frame is to be covered with cloth, it is not necessary to web the back to support the cover. However, if the frame is deeper than one inch, the webbing could be well used and at little added expense.

Solid Base Backs—The same methods apply to any type of padding used on solid wood backs, as were described in the previous sections on seats.

Outdoor Backs—The same methods and precautions apply here as they do in the section of outdoor seats.

Automobile Backs—There is little difference in the construction of the vertical seat member of an automobile seat. Its shape is somewhat different but the actual construction is no different. The material, springs and attachments are identical and must hold the same amount of applied force. For more specific information see the previous section concerned with automobile seats.

Top Edges for Backs—In many styles of upholstery none of the wood frame shows at the sides or the top of the backs. The flat wooden sides can be covered easily with fabric but the top must have a consideration for padded comfort. There are several methods of accomplishing this, as shown in Fig. 44:

the square, slightly padded; the over-roll; the scroll back; the slant or knife edge; and several others. If, in some cases, the finished wooden edge is left as decoration, it must be completely finished before the upholstery is begun.

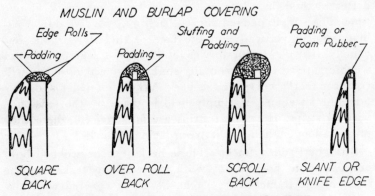

Figure 44—Types of Top Edges for Backs

Wing Backs—Since the beginning of the age of comfortable seating furniture, the winged side or back has been popular. Almost all of the winged backs are confined to easy chairs. For those who plan to reupholster a unit which has this type of back the covering process will be explained later. The web-

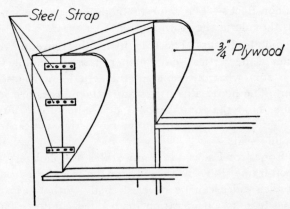

Figure 45—Wings Added to Straight Back Chair

bing is usually placed on the front of the wing and some sort of padding applied over it, either foam rubber or cotton and fiber. In cases where the wing is big enough the small diameter coil springs can be used along with webbing on the back of the wing frame. The sagless spring is much too stiff a mem-

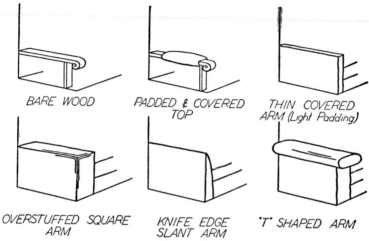

BARE WOOD

PADDED & COVERED TOP

THIN COVERED ARM (Light Padding)

OVERSTUFFED SQUARE ARM

KNIFE EDGE SLANT ARM

'T' SHAPED ARM

Figure 46—Some Standard Types of Arms

ber for this application. The addition of a wing can be effected by the use of a solid piece of ¾″ plywood securely fastened with dowels or steel straps as shown in Fig. 45. This can be done at the same time the arm rest is stripped or enlarged. If it is desired to take off existing wing sections, first examine to see whether or not they constitute a bracing member. If not, they can be sawed off and the holes left unfilled, if they are to be covered with upholstery. In larger pieces of overstuffed furniture the wings may be so big and involve so much padding that they might better be made up of framing as is the rest of the chair and securely dowelled, glued and braced in place. Wing sections must take a great deal of stress and strain.

Arms

One of the most difficult elements to treat properly in all furniture is the arm piece. In much modern furniture the arms

are either left off or they are plain bare wood. In the past there
have been as many types of arms as there have been furniture
craftsmen. Some of the more popular types are shown in Fig.
46. If you are in the process of reupholstery, it is very important to check the solidity of the arm structure. Since it gets
perhaps the most stress and strain, it is apt to be unglued and
in need of repair. In some cases the arms may be removed
completely or cut down. But again a word of caution about the
arms when they are used as a bracing member; if there is a
doubt in your mind about the application of the arm, **do not
remove it.**

Enclosed Overstuffed Arm Rests—Many of the types of
padded arms have been outmoded by high cost, good taste, and
utility. Of the most popular types in this element are the
square, set back square, slope set back, block square, round or
scroll, Lawson, slant or knife edge, and the "T" shape. All
these types are built and padded around a wooden frame, the
size of which depends upon the final configuration desired.
The actual process for covering and upholstering these arms
will be shown later in this book. When the arm rest remains
un-upholstered, then it must be finished before any upholstering is started or at least before the final covering is reapplied
over the muslin undercover. The webbing of these stuffed units
are completed from the front. Seldom are coil springs used in
these sections due to the small space involved. Solid burlap or
standard webbing can be used and the tension need not be
too tight. If the outside of the arm section is to be covered
with material down to the base, then it might be well to place
semi-tight webbing of good quality in the vertical direction on
the outside of the unit. This will prevent fabric dents caused
by inward stretching from some exterior blow.

Outdoor Furniture—Usually the frame of the porch piece
or the back yard divan is painted wood or formed metal. If it
is desired to have a padded arm rest, at least on the top of the
arm, then the use of sealed foam rubber, coated hair or fiber
is the best stuffing. Cotton is not recommended. The same precautions must be observed for furniture which will be used in
the basement recreation room during the humid summer

months. During the heating season any type of furniture can be used in the basement area.

Automobile Arm Rests—One of the most frequent points of upholstery wear in an automobile is the arm rest on either front door. These units are most always some form of sponge rubber and often the upholstery is sewn in shape and glued on to the rubber. In this case I would suggest the replacement of the arm rest unless it is unavailable. If it is not possible to remove the arm rest without taking the door apart, then I would suggest that the fabric be sewn in shape and applied with either glue or stitches pulled through the rubber with the long upholsterer's needle.

Baby Carriages—The sides or arm bumpers of most good carriages have some form of upholstery. It is placed on a solid board and tacked, glued or stapled in place. These units can be easily removed and recovered with a waterproof fabric. If the stuffing is missing then it is advisable to obtain some kapok, which is moisture resistant, and repad with at least ½" thick compresses.

Edging or Edge Rolls

These have been mentioned in the earlier part of the text, but not much was said about the home constructed edge roll and its infinite number of variations possible for different applications. The general purpose of these rolls is to make a definite edge which will not deform under use. The rolls can be used to fill out sections of the furniture to give it a new shape. The pre-made shapes do not come in enough variety to be generally applicable in any cases but simple edge forming, such as around seat fronts, arm rests, wing fronts and other places where round edges might be useful. When a different edge or shape is needed, the edge roll must be fabricated from a piece of good burlap and hair or fiber stuffing (some non-destructable or crushable material—cotton would not be satisfactory). The bottom flap of any of these rolls must be securely tacked or stapled to the frame and the hair or fiber must be tightly rolled into it. Fig. 47 illustrates edge roll application. If there are any soft spots (lack of padding) the edge will tend to flatten out permanently.

Sponge Rubber and Foam Rubber—These materials make exceptionally fine edge rolls but are hard to form in other than round shapes. The diameter of the largest round fibre or hair roll is about 1½" while the rubber rolls can be made much larger and will never break down. The burlap is tacked or

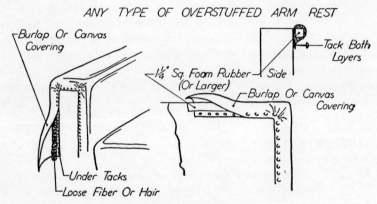

Figure 47—Hand-made Edge Rolls for Any Type of Overstuffed Arm Rest

stapled in the same fashion. The rubber is rolled into the bur lap and the other edge tacked down. The rubber may be cut in square lengths or strips according to the size of roll desired. The length or strip of rubber should be at least ½ inch larger in thickness than the roll desired. Thus when the roll is confined, there will be no sharp edges.

Chapter 6

OPERATIONS

Webbing

Jute Strap, Burlap, and Steel (strap and wire lath) have been mentioned previously in the text just enough to give you a working familiarity with them. From this point the

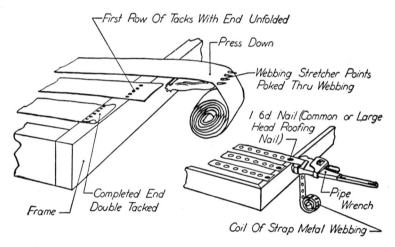

Figure 48—Webbing Application

definite steps for the applications of these webbing materials is just an explanation away.

Jute (Burlap) Strap—The most familiar of all the webbing is the conventional strap type. It can be obtained in several qualities and of several strengths and widths, but from experience it is wisest to use the heaviest grade and the best quality you can buy. It comes in rolls from 25 to 1000 feet in length. In calculating the correct length for your project, first figure the number of webbing sections that will be needed (never spacing them closer than ½″, usually about 1″). For each section add about 4″ so that over all you will have enough extra strap to use as a pulling end. The spiked end of the webbing stretcher tool is poked into this to give added leverage when tensioning the jute webbing, as shown in Fig. 48.

As the jute is first applied to the side of the frame bottom it is best to use the special webbing tacks or heavy duty cleated staples (from staple gun). The webbing tacks also have retaining cleats to secure them in place. Pound in only **four** tacks in the first layer, leaving at least one inch to fold back, and tack with four or five tacks. Placing the rubber **or** padded end of the stretcher against the frame after inserting the points into the webbing, pull down, tensioning the strap. Too much tension is worse than too little. When you begin to see the jute pull against the tack heads then fasten the strap. Now fold back an inch from the end you have just used to tension with the webbing stretcher and tack again, as shown in Fig. 48. After the strap has been completely tacked, cut the strapping at the point ½″ away from the tacks. **Do not pre-cut any of the webbing pieces, since you must have extra length in which to insert the webbing stretcher.** Continue placing all the parallel straps of webbing until the one direction is completed.

The jute webbing is always woven to give it a more uniform resistance to the pressures exerted on it. A solid piece of **flat burlap webbing** is not used on the bottom of a chair, but rather in the seat or on the arms and the tension may be effected by hand strength in many cases. On some seats there are tensioning springs. The cross section areas of the webbing must be stitched or sewed, but this can wait until the position of the coil springs has been decided.

Steel strapping—This is a useful type of webbing providing there is sufficient strength in the frame to hold the nails or screws which secure the strapping. The webbing stretcher used on this type of material is a special tool and must be purchased for this purpose. However, a plumber's sharp-jawed pipe wrench with a block of wood will work just as well, providing you do not distort the frame with too much leverage.

Wire Lath—A new use for this material has met with great success, since it does not stretch or distort. The holes in the lath provide all the possible places on which the coil springs can be fastened with clips, wire, etc. It is a good idea to place a piece of insulating burlap between the lath and the coil springs before they are fastened down.

Coil Spring Planning

There is not one size or strength of coil spring which will work for all applications. It is only logical to assume that the larger the number of coils in the seat the greater the division of weight. Also, the greater the weight of the load the more care that must be exercised in the choice of the springs. You will find that there are several to choose from; the heavier springs are used in the seats and the lighter ones in the backs. If you are unable to get precisely the correct spring size, choose the next smallest size of stronger spring wire. It that is not available, choose the next size larger than the one you need but with less spring strength. When retying old spring units do not use the old twine, no matter how strong it may seem. The methods of tying will be discussed later in this chapter.

Seat Coil Arrangements—The coils used without spring steel edge wire must clear the inside of the frame by at least 2″ so that in compressing they will not rub the wood. The tops of the coils should be no closer than 1½″ apart when in position and tied. For most seat applications the top of the center springs should not be higher than 3″, and not tied down less than 2½″ above the frame top (see Fig. 49). All coil springs should be "circled" at the top so that there is no chance for a loose end to poke through the paddings. The formed top wire of the spring coils should be bent over and fastened around its own loop. The springs are applied to the bottom webbing or solid base first by the use of stitches through the jute, or staples or clamps into the solid wooden base. A pair of hog ring pliers and the open rings can be used to crimp the bottom spring to the jute webbing or to either of the steel products. This is a most useful tool for all wire fastening. There are special clamps available for this purpose but are somewhat expensive. The steel "hog rings" do not come apart easily and

can be used to clamp fabric and materials together for tempo-
rary holding while stitching. In most cases they will eliminate
the necessity of the long skewer or the upholsterer's pin.

Planning the Number of Springs—Both dimensions of the
area should be first divided in half, then the resulting four
quadrants judged for spring space. All springs must be two

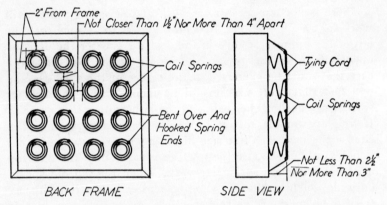

Figure 49—Coil Spring Application

inches from the edge (see Fig. 49). If the unit is to have a
spring steel edge wire at the front of the seat or cushion, the
front row should be made up of shorter springs having greater
strength so as to hold up the wire edge. Corner torsion springs
may be added as in Fig. 6, to hold the shape of the corner.
Measuring and bending the edge wire will be discussed later
in this chapter.

Spring Tying for Seats—The single most important factor
in the final form of the seating section is the tying of the
springs. The tying accomplishes one thing; it fixes the spring
tops in a position where they cannot shift, causing a drop in
the padding or, as often happens with old or poor twine, the
spring breaking loose and finally popping up out of the cover.
The twine used is specially made for this purpose and there
is no real lasting substitute, though many cords may look like
the same thing. There are two major methods or systems of
tying; the two-way tie and the four-way tie. In the two-way

tie method, the cord goes through the center of each coil
spring and is loop-tied around each edge and then to the frame.
The four-way tie starts the same way as the two-way tie.
Then, as these right angle cords are tied in place the diagonal
cords are tied in, thus dividing the circle formed by each coil
top into eight sections. The latter makes a much more substantial seat and is best for most purposes, but where a soft

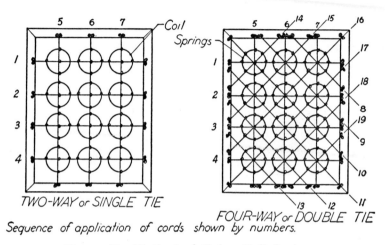

TWO-WAY or SINGLE TIE

FOUR-WAY or DOUBLE TIE

Sequence of application of cords shown by numbers.

Figure 50—Method of Tying Coil Springs

seat is needed the two-way tie is sufficient. The coil springs
around the edge can either be tied in place with the tops flat,
thus forming a flat seat, or they can be pulled to a slanted (45°)
position in preparation for a rounded seat. The same method
will be shown for back spring structures so that both pleated
barrel chairs and round formed edges can be formed. The two-
way and four-way methods of tying springs and edges are
shown in Fig. 50.

Marshall Units—Since these spring units are encapsulated
in cloth sacks and sewn in long strips there is little problem
in sewing them together in a wider or more rectangular unit.
However, in using these units you will find that they are
smaller springs, of less strength and must have a shallower
frame. It is possible to install them by exactly the same procedure as described for the seat coil springs. The Marshall

units are a favorite for cushions, and they are also used for mattresses and other heavy duty work. The cloth, canvas or muslin sack makes the springs easy to handle and to form, and everything that can be done with the separate spring can be done with the Marshall unit, with the exception that more springs must be used. The tying of the bagged units is accomplished by using a heavy upholsterer's needle.

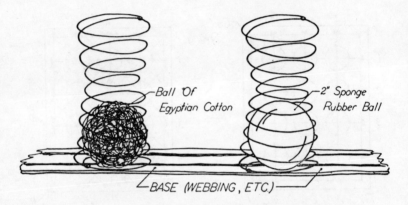

Figure 51—Method of Sound Proofing Coil Springs

Sound Proofing Coil Springs—Sometimes when coil units are installed over a solid base the springs make noise, using their base as a sounding board. This can be eliminated by the installation of a small amount of Egyptian cotton or a chunk of foam rubber. A small sponge rubber ball 2″ in diameter will also effect the same quietness (see Fig. 51).

Spring Steel Wire

For the person who has had little experience with the fabrication of spring steel wire, it will be a difficult job to straighten, cut, bend and fit this wire. The best bet for edge wire is to insist on absolutely straight sections which can be notched at the right length and broken by simple bending with the bending tool and a heavy pair of pliers. To try to cut hardened steel would be a waste of good tools and time. In bending any of this edge wire it is best to obtain two 12″ pieces of ⅜″ or ¼″ iron water pipe as a bending sleeve (see Fig. 52). There can be no heating of this spring wire to temporarily remove the temper since it can only be restored by expert techniques. Spring wire can be cut with a standard bolt cutter, but not side cutting pliers or the like. Hardened metal will ruin any standard cutting edge. Heavy wire (#9 and larger) can also be cut with an aluminum oxide disc on a table saw or grinding wheel.

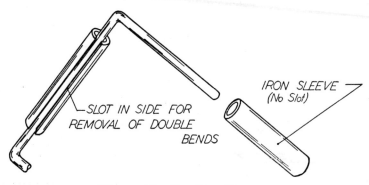

Figure 52—Bending Sleeves

Binding Edge Wire and Other Units—As has been mentioned before, the hog ring pliers and clamp rings afford the most universal method of clamping two joining wires together. However, there are standard clamps and binding wire available for the same job, and may be applied in the manner shown in Fig. 53. Again, do not try to weld, braze or solder these spring wires together—retempering is impossible for the amateur.

Spring Backs—In many instances the back is the most difficult to effect in a correct manner, due to the fact that the back must give more easily in the center and be somewhat more rigid in the border areas. The springs used can either be separate coil springs or Marshall units. The coil springs, when used separately, should be about five inches apart unless the back area is too small. The spring strength must be slightly less than that of the seat springs. Edge wire or stiffer springs can be used around the border. If back springs of two strengths are not available, it is possible to strengthen the edge or border springs by four-way tying. The webbing for

either coil springs or Marshall units will be applied to the
back of the frame, but the vertical webbing strips can be
tacked to the inside of the frame.

Tying Back Springs

If the back springs were to be completely tied by the four-
way method, the back would be too stiff for comfort. It is
possible to tie the springs lightly to each other and then cover

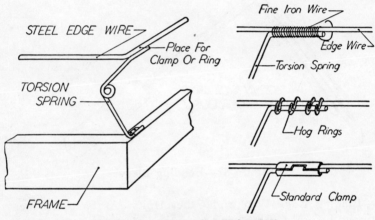

Figure 53—Clamping Edge Wire

the complete back with a heavy grade of jute burlap to which
the top coils of the spring can be sewn for support. Since the
back gets little heavy wear the burlap will act to hold the
springs in place, provided they are not tensioned too tightly
(3 to 5 inches above the frame surface). If Marshall units
are used, many more springs will be included. The back frame
must be boarded up so that the shorter Marshall units stick
out only 2 to 3 inches past the frame surface. A general burlap
covering can then be applied over the units and stitched in
place. All springs, regardless of their tying and construction
on the back or seats, must be covered with some form of "insulator" to keep the springs from poking through. Then they
should be padded either with rubberized fibre, cotton, foam
rubber or other material. The art of padding is very important
since any variations are especially noticeable when the unit
is in use.

Padding and Edging

There are two layers of stuffing used in most soft seats, whether they are built on a solid board base, tight webbing (no springs), or on springs of any sort. The burlap covering over the foundation unit (springs, etc.) has to be tacked or stapled in place. The edge roll or edging must be tacked in place also so that the unit is ready for two layers of fibre

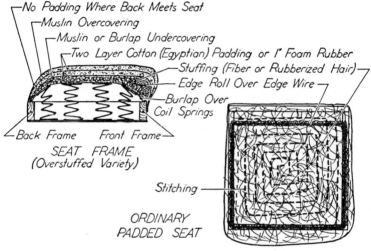

Figure 54—Padding and Stuffing Methods

padding. After the edge roll is in place, the first layer of stuffing or padding is applied by pulling the rubberized fibre or animal hair apart into smooth shreds without clumps or foreign matter. The first layer is applied rather densely, especially around the borders where it meets the edge roll. The first layer must be stitched in place by long loose stitches which proceed from the outer edge and run in lines parallel to the edges, decreasing as they go toward the center, as shown in Fig. 54. The second layer should be of a finer grade of hair or felt (rubberized or not) and layed somewhat looser than the first layer of fibres or hair. It need not be stitched or, if desired, the stitches should not be pulled down tight.

Padding and Stuffing for Heavy Coil and Sagless Springs— In many cases there is no edge roll, instead the padding in several layers is counted upon to give a true rounded appearance to the edges of the piece. In these cases an "insulator" is applied over the burlap spring cover. The padding (one inch foam rubber or two layers of Egyptian cotton over one inch of fibre stuffing) is put in place and covered with plastic impregnated muslin, or plain muslin if foam rubber is not used (see Fig. 54).

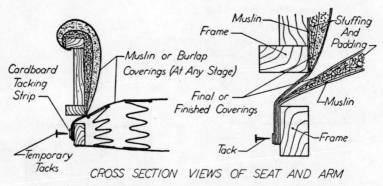

CROSS SECTION VIEWS OF SEAT AND ARM

Figure 55—Tacking of Joining Side to Seat Material

The final covering is then applied over all and tacked in place. All upholstery should be started from the interior of the unit, that is, the seating area as opposed to the outside of the arms or back. In this way the various coverings can be tacked in joining places so as to form tight, smooth covered sections (see Fig. 55).

Muslin covering of all padded areas—After the stuffing or padding has been sewn in place in any one of the different areas, it is wise to cover that section with muslin and fasten down all edges, except where it must be joined with another piece of muslin from another area. These sections (where the seat and arm or back coverings meet) must wait until the final covering has been applied and the full section can be tacked at the same time (see Fig. 55). There may be four sections of cloth tacked at these joints. Usually you can secure or tack one of the muslin sections, but it is best to wait until the final inside covering has been applied. In some reupholstery jobs it may be necessary to remove the tacks holding the covers in these sections, but this will not loosen the remainder of the muslin covering.

Final Covering Material

Previously I have discussed some of the factors which govern the choice of final covering material. The following discussion is intended to expand your consideration of the possibilities of the correct choice for each piece or for any application.

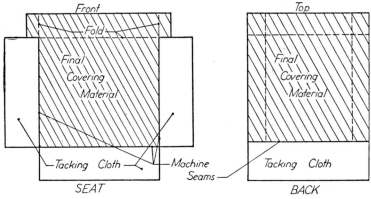

Figure 56—Application of Tacking Cloths

The furniture which graces the usual living room must be both durable and decorative. If there are children to use this furniture then the covering must be chosen with them in mind. Often the choice of durable pure plastics, while not quite so soft in their decorative appearance, are quite child proof. The material for removable covers should be cotton and washable. The cloths of various types include denim, sail cloth, twill (any design), both glazed or unglazed chintz, and pebble cloths. Linen grade canvas makes a fine covering of lifetime durability but is somewhat more expensive than most other types of covering cloth. Those fabrics which are intended for service in less wearing duty are any of the wool nubby cloths, boucle (looped end cloth), tapestry (needlepoint, pettipoint), repp (corded fabric, squared off raised cords) and wool Damask. Some of the newer fabrics include glass fiber woven cloth of remarkable durability (in many permanent colors) metallic cloth (aluminum, magnesium alloy, etc.) and plastic woven fabric in many colors and weaves.

Most of the better materials can be spared by the use of sail cloth or heavy denim as sewn on tacking cloths (see Fig. 56). The area to be covered by the cushion may also be a sewn on piece of denim rather than the expensive upholstery material. Hence, wherever it is necessary to tack down a piece of material, and that section will not be seen, other cloth may be sewn in place to serve.

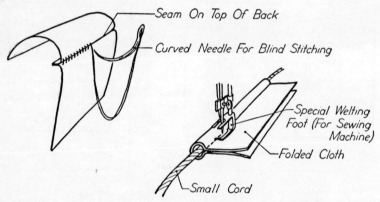

Figure 57—Method of Making Welting

Sewing

The application of the needle, whether by hand or by machine, will "make" or "break" the upholstery project. Fig. 15 shows the different types of needles used in the trade. All of them are not necessary, but I would suggest that two sizes of curved needles are necessary for stitching on a right angle corner where there is no chance to reach the back side, and two or three sizes of large needles, at least one with the eye at the point for quick heavy lacing. The eye in this type of needle is usually open on one side for easy thread removal after each stitch.

In upholstery there are several important functions served by sewing; holding pieces of cloth together, keeping stuffing or padding in place, and helping a padding or stuffing formed section keep its shape. Welts are desirable to keep the sharp edges of the cushion, seat or arm, etc., from wearing out. This welting is usually stitched on a machine, due to the heavy nature of the cloth, but hand sewing can be effected easily with the correct needle. Welting is made by covering any diameter cord with either the same cloth or different (for contrast), and sewing the two flaps tightly around the cord leaving these flaps (¾" each) to be sewn to the joining sections of covering (shown to the right in Fig. 57).

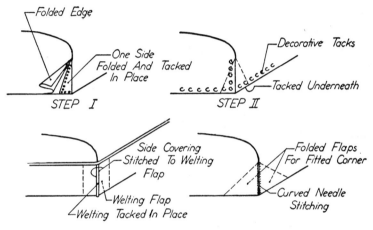

Figure 58—Corner Types

Machine Sewing—Most makes of sewing machines include in their instructions specific information for the sewing of heavy cloth and plastic (including leather and leatherette). Contrary to common belief, heavy materials can be sewn on the ordinary home machine, providing the proper settings are made on the machine. There are special needles for leather and plastic coated cloth. Ordinary thread may be used in most cases of cloth sewing, but heavier grades must be used on heavier material.

Tying Knots—The application of several knots in tying springs together and sewing the top coil of the springs to the burlap covering is standard practice in upholstery. These knots must be made with care to guard against their coming loose.

Corners—These present a problem in finished neatness which can be easily overcome by practice with unimportant pieces of cloth on the corner in question. The most used types of corners include the folded and stitched corner, the folded and tacked corner, the "blind" sewn and fitted corner and the corner formed with welting. These are illustrated in Fig. 58.

Blind Stitching—It is often necessary to sew in places where there would be no possibility of sewing, if the piece of covering (all but the remaining row of stitches) were in place. Thus with blind sewing these stitches are sewn first from the other side, then the flap of cloth is put in place and tacked or sewn. Fig. 59 shows examples of this so-called "blind" stitching.

Pull Stitching—The uses for pull stitching come to light when it is necessary to form a curved scroll covering or extra tight curved section where there is not sufficient cloth to pull with an ordinary stretcher. The thread is inserted with a curved needle around the curved section and pulled tight much

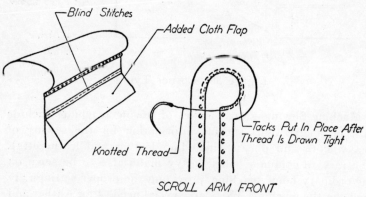

SCROLL ARM FRONT

Figure 59—Blind Stitching

in the fashion of a draw string, then the cloth can be tacked in place. Other applications include pulling a "blind" seam down into a space between two sections of a piece of furniture, and for holding together two parts of a covering while smaller hidden stitches are inserted either with or without welting (see Fig. 59).

Chapter 7

PROJECT ELEMENTS—SEATS

Types of Seats

Rather than develop any single project through its many steps and then proceed to other projects which include many of the same steps, I have sought to simplify the explanation of these steps by treating them as different project elements which can be used in any project where they are needed. Every piece of upholstered furniture has a seat, and there are only a few different methods for upholstering seats. Almost every piece has a back; some with upholstery, others without. The same can be said for every other element such as arms, wings, cushions, padded facings, etc. As I develop these elements, remember that any one of these descriptions is not intended to constitute a fully upholstered unit. When one arm is fully described the alternate arm would naturally be upholstered in the same manner. This same procedure will be followed through the rest of the project elements.

Chair (Dining Type With Straight Back and No Arms)

The simplest beginning is the ordinary chair, without arms and with various types of backs. Without a back this chair becomes a bench or stool, but the seat upholstery is done the same way. In all cases in this explanation we will consider the chair as the frame shown in Fig. 60 and the various types of seats will be carried from there.

Strung Webbing Support—Part I of Fig. 60 shows the jute webbing applied in a woven manner to the top of the seat frame. The webbing is spaced with at least ½ inch and not more than 1¼ inches between strips. The webbing should be done all in one direction first, one strip at a time, cutting the webbing only after it has been stretched and tacked. The webbing can then be woven in the other direction into the already tensioned and tacked strips. Care must be taken to insure the

identical tension on each webbing strip; none must be tighter
or looser than the others. Padding cannot cover this type of
mistake; everytime you sit on the chair or stool it will be
immediately noticeable.

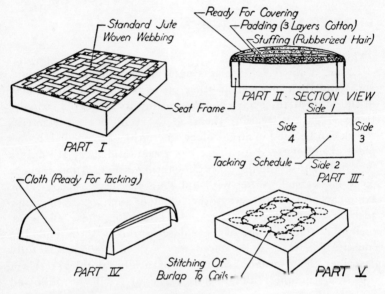

Figure 60—Upholstering Process for Seat

Edging, Padding and Stuffing—Part II of Fig. 60 shows the
layer construction of the edging, padding and stuffing. The
edging is applied after the webbing has been covered with a
section of burlap cloth. It is possible to use overhanging flaps
of the burlap covering rolled over hair or fiber stuffing to form
the edge roll. After the edge roll is applied in place and
stitched to prevent its stuffing from slipping, the first layer of
hair can be applied and stitched in place. The second layer, as
shown in Part II of Fig. 60, comes up and raises in the center
of the seat so as to make a smooth approach to the edge roll.
Over all, several layers of Egyptian cotton padding may be
applied. To avoid sharp square edges, the cotton should be
torn off the roll rather than cut. Pulling tends to thin out the
edges for a smoother job. When the padding and stuffing have

been oriented so as to be free from lumps and depressions, a covering of muslin may be added to hold them in place. Start by tacking one side, then stretch and tack the opposite side as shown in Part III of Fig. 60, making sure to stretch the cloth evenly in all directions. The other two sides should be tacked and stretched in the same fashion. Corners on the muslin cover may be notched out or folded, then tacked in place.

Final Covering—The final covering should be measured after the muslin covering has been applied. The general size of the square or rectangle of the cloth should be large enough to extend well around and under the frame (see Fig. 60, Part IV). The tacking method is the same as with the muslin cover with the exception of the corners. They should be left untacked until the final step, after all sides are tacked.

Webbing for Coil Springs—If it is desired to use coil springs, then the webbing must be applied to the bottom of the frame; in this case, the same frame as in Part I of Fig. 60. The webbing is attached, woven and tacked in the same manner but webbing tacks with cleats are used.

Installing the Coil Springs—The layout of the coils is shown in Figs. 49 and 50. The tying of the bottom of the coil is accomplished first either by sewing the spring wire in place or by the use of hog rings. When the type of seat has been chosen, the tying of the top of the coils together must be done (see Fig. 50). Two-way tying produces a softer seat than does the four-way tie. Part V of Fig. 60 shows the spring installation and tying in the ordinary frame. Burlap or heavy canvas can be used as an "insulator" and for top covering of the coil springs.

Edging, Padding, and Stuffing—There is little difference between the upholstery of the coil spring unit and the simple webbing support foundation after the springs have been tied and the spring cover tacked and sewn in place. Foam rubber may be substituted for all layers of padding.

Final Covering—The same process of covering can be followed in the case of the spring unit as was described earlier for the simple webbing support foundation.

Upholstery on Solid Bases—In some cases a solid base is better than the simple webbing support foundation. Where the reinforcement of the added wooden frame top is necessary, the padding and upholstery are little different than the simple frame upholstery without springs. In these cases the best padding and stuffing material has proved to be foam rubber. The wooden base must be drilled for ventilation before the padding is applied. In the cases where ordinary padding, stuffing and covering is used, treat the work as described earlier in this chapter on the simple webbed frame.

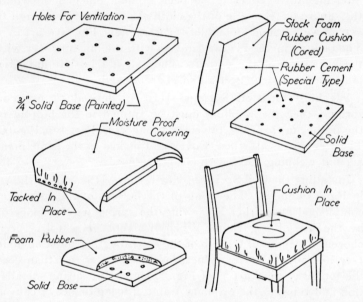

Figure 61—Method of Upholstering Solid Base with Foam Rubber Padding

Foam Rubber Padding—The base should be prepared before the application of the foam rubber by the application of a coat of paint to seal the solid base board. If the chair or seat is to be used where there is moisture, then a thin layer of aluminum foil is suggested as a base for the foam rubber over the wood (see Fig. 42). The foam rubber can be simply tacked in place or may be glued with moisture proof cement. The edges should be tacked in place before the plastic impregnated muslin is put over the rubber as a moisture and odor proofing barrier.

This muslin is tacked in place and the corners made up exactly like the usual muslin covering as previously described. Fig. 61 shows method of upholstering the solid base with foam rubber padding.

In the case of the "overstuffed" or occasional chair, certain problems arise due to the addition of arms or a back which are connected onto the seat frame. These problems in the main

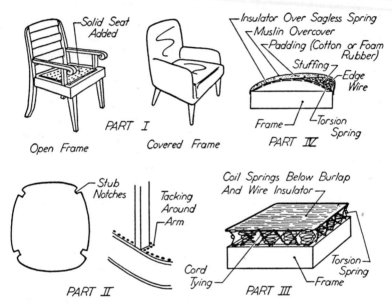

Figure 62—Seat Upholstery for Overstuffed Chair

Chair (Overstuffed, With Open or Upholstered Back)

are concerned with the proper fitting of the upholstery around arms and backs in a smooth and neat fashion. The "occasional" chair usually has arms and back upright supports which are not covered or upholstered. The "overstuffed" chair or sofa presents problems of two sections of padded and stuffed upholstery meeting as well as arm sections which may be either bare wood or upholstered. These two chairs are illustrated in Part I of Fig. 62. In this type of furniture the simple webbing support foundation is seldom used. Therefore, we will deal directly with those differences which exist between the simple frame chair seat and those already mentioned in this section, still concentrating on the seat area. Those methods which have been described will not be repeated but reference will be given to them.

Webbing and Coil Springs—It will be found that most existing furniture employs this type of construction and upholstery. The seat frame need not be treated any differently than the simple chair frame even though the larger unit may involve a seat twice as wide and five times as long. If webbing and coil spring construction is to be used, follow the method for the layout already shown in Figs. 42, 48, 49, 50, 51, and 60. Since the seating area has the most tension on the spring area, the burlap covering can be tacked in place over the coils after they are tied (see Fig. 50). Where arms are attached to the frame, the covering can be cut or notched out and tacked in place around the arm as was shown in Fig. 62, Part II. Where other elements of upholstery must meet the seat covering (arms, backs, etc.), the seat should not be carried any further than the burlap spring cover.

Sagless Spring—The important point in the application of sagless springs is to make sure that the frame is strong enough to withstand the strain imposed upon it by the spring units. When the sagless springs are installed and the seat is sat upon, the weight and force is not taken up by the springs and the webbing. It is transferred to the frame directly. If the frame unit is not strong enough or the spring cleats not fastened securely into the frame, the complete job may fail and have to be done over. Bracing can be effected in those spots where the most tension will be distributed (see Figs. 32 and 33). The tables for the calculations for the proper choice of the sagless spring for the frame size have been given previously in the first chapter of the book. When the sagless spring is used within a frame and no edge wire is planned then the "insulator" can be placed over the installed springs and tacked in place ready for further padding and stuffing. Where the seat has the application of edge wire to form out the front and/or sides of the seat, the "insulator" and tying must be followed as shown in Fig. 62 (previous references to these elements are made in Figs. 5 and 6).

Edging for Platform Seat—In many pieces of stuffed furniture the seat cushion is removable and therefore there must be some sort of padding over the spring units or a platform for the cushion. Usually the front of the seat is padded with either an edge roll or some form of rubber formed edging (see Figs. 25 and 47). When this is desired over the sagless spring construction, edge wire makes the most easily adaptable final edge construction with the muslin covering over the "insulator" and the edge roll. When the final covering is applied, a piece of canvas or denim should be sewn to the piece of fabric covering (upholstery cloth) which will cover only the front edge.

Padding and Stuffing—There is little difference in the underpadding and stuffing of sagless spring units. The use of the "insulator" is necessary to prevent the spring from being felt through the finished upholstery. Where cotton padding or foam rubber is used on a unit having edge wire construction and sagless springs, the use of rubberized hair or fiber is advised to pad out the space between the curved springs and the edge wire padding (see Fig. 62). Over this can be applied either cotton (three layers) or one-inch foam rubber. Over either of these is stretched and tacked the muslin or canvas undercovering as has been described earlier in this chapter.

Where the foam rubber must be fitted around arm or back stubs or members the notch in the foam rubber should be cut about ½ inch smaller in all directions so that the rubber will fit close and smooth and can be fastened in place (see Fig. 62). Tacking tape should be glued to the edge of the foam rubber in order that it can be tacked in place with a smooth edge of any desired curvature. Since foam rubber comes in several densities, it is wise to refer to the directions of the manufacturer for the correct one for any particular application. For simple solid foam rubber padding, the larger the area the denser should be the rubber.

Solid Wood Seat Bases and Hollow Core Foam Rubber—Foam rubber is manufactured in many thicknesses but seldom is solid in thicknesses over two inches. When it is desired to use this material in greater thickness, it must be either cored stock (see Figs. 12 and 13) or stock composed of several thicknesses glued together (see Fig. 63). Trimming and shaping of

the edges is possible providing certain precautions are re-
garded, as will be explained in this section. The solid base
must be of sufficient strength to support whatever weight it
will be required to hold. It should be drilled for ventilation and
securely fastened to the existing frame (see Fig. 61).

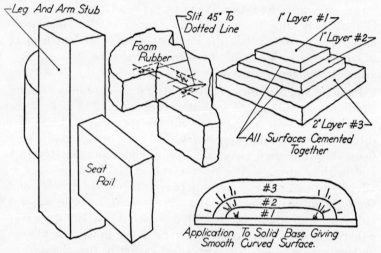

Figure 63—Method of Making Foam Rubber Seat

Covering Foam Rubber—As has been explained before,
foam rubber must have a moisture proofing cover applied to
its surface. This can either be plastic impregnated cloth or
Saran plastic (a very durable and moisture proof plastic).
Over this undercover, which has been tacked in place, can be
applied the final upholstery covering.

The final covering must be fitted around the arm stubs or
members with either folded edges or welting (see Figs. 56 to
58). If the unit involved is a piece of furniture which has a
cover, back or arm section, then it is best to defer the final
covering until all sections have been webbed, sprung padded
and undercovered.

Foam Rubber With Air Pocket (Sealed Air)—Standard
sized units made of foam rubber containing sealed-in air
pockets can be purchased for cushioning and padding. These

units provide thicker padding with less weight and cannot be cut. Various types of shapes can be obtained from the manufacturers (see Figs. 13 and 64). Once punctured or cut into, these units will lose their weight supporting ability. To avoid this, smaller units built up with pieces of other foam rubber should be used for a special shape.

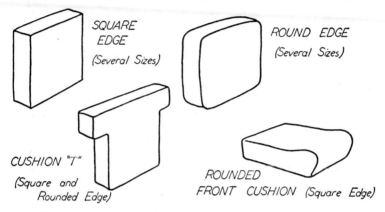

Figure 64—Standard Seat Cushions of Foam Rubber Containing Sealed-In Air Pocket

To review the methods of cutting, shaping and gluing foam rubber would be a wise move before beginning any project involving this material.

Foam rubber may be cut by using an ordinary bread knife which has fine teeth or a rough edge. It also may be cut with a pair of heavy tailor's shears or by a motor driven band saw using a fine-tooth metal cutting blade, which has very little set to its teeth (at least 24 teeth to an inch).

The work surface should be clean and sprinkled with talc or powdered soapstone. This provides a surface which does not allow the foam rubber to adhere causing incorrect cuts and measurements. The surface should be both flat and level, being large enough to effect whatever gluing of larger pieces together is necessary. Often, when the length of a couch must be covered with foam rubber, there must be several pieces fitted together and glued solidly. When using cut pieces of

cored stock it is best to plan to cover the wide edges with a
long strip of one-inch thick foam rubber and securely glue it
in place, as shown in Fig. 65. If a crown or convex shape is

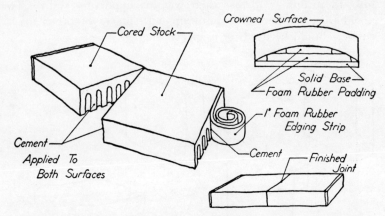

**Figure 65—Method of Joining Separate Pieces of Cored
Foam Rubber**

desired in the seat, then sections of foam rubber padding may
be added in the center of the cored unit between the webbing,
springs or other support base. This extra padding will not be
definable in the finished product but will give the raised effect
(see Fig. 65).

Chapter 8

PROJECT ELEMENTS—ARMS

Types of Arms

As has been previously suggested, arms present special problems in the upholstering of various pieces of furniture. In this chapter I will show the most common types of arm presentations. Whatever changes might be necessary in your particular project probably will be simple adaptations of these

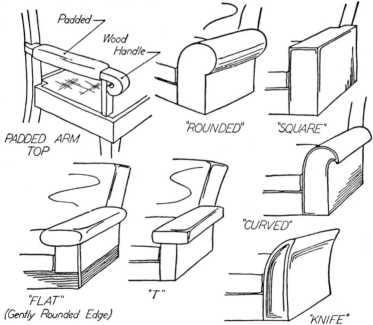

Figure 66—Various Types of Arms

types. Many modern pieces of furniture have open arms with only top padding or no padding at all. The overstuffed sectional sofa may have no arm sections or simply a solid block arm rest which is recessed back from the front of the seat. In Fig. 66 are sketched the various types of arms which are con-

sidered most commonly used. In most of the arm applications
in overstuffed furniture where there are two sets of springs
used, one in the frame and another (Marshall unit) in the
cushion, the arms are of the padded variety. In these cases the
arm padding and edge rolls can be added after the seat work
has been all but covered. Where the seat springing and padding extend above the beginning of the arm padding or edge
rolls, then the arm must be underpadded first.

Wide Top (Lawson Type, Both Sides Covered and Padded)
—In the majority of the cases in overstuffed and single seat
units, the arms are of the completely padded type. They may
appear as the rounded, flat, "T" shaped flat, curved, square, or
any of the others, but all are constructed in the same manner.
The arm structure is usually of heavy design having open
framework with wide top surfaces. The open frame must be
webbed or covered so as to support the padding and covering
without a chance of inward "denting" (that is, stretching the
final cloth with dents by an accidental push inward). The construction of these arms is usually small enough so that they
need not be sprung or webbed with anything but ordinary jute
webbing. The edge rolls are applied in the same manner as
described previously. The understuffing is installed and tacked
at random in order to hold the first layer of fiber or hair in
place. Subsequent layers of stuffing and padding are added as
was explained in other sections.

Knife Edge—In "period" furniture the "Knife" edge has
been a very popular type of arm rest, though not too comfortable for prolonged resting. The "Knife" edge is one of the
hardest types of arm upholstery to effect (see Figs. 67 and 70).
Its surface goes from the wide bottom next to the seat up in a
gentle curve to the fairly sharp edge at the top. This gentle
edge must be resilient and still curve upwards. Ordinary webbing will only hold a very gentle curve. If the space is too
small or not strong enough for sagless springs, then one or two
coil springs are suggested to keep pressure on the webbing
from the back. Wire lath may be used in this case, if it can be
supported from the back by coil springs. The padding, stuffing
and covering can be accomplished in the same manner as with
other elements of upholstery previously described.

Scroll, or Curved Top—The only major problem in the curved or scroll top arm is fitting the covering around the front of the arm so that a front covered and padded templet

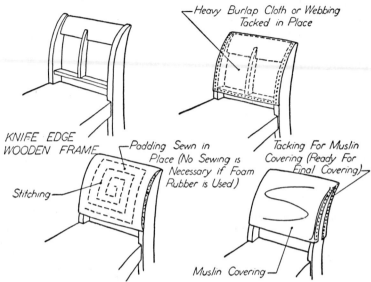

Figure 67—"Knife Edge" Arm

can be added. The coverings, both the muslin and the final upholstery, are to be stretched first over the arm from the top down. Then they are stretched over the padding and

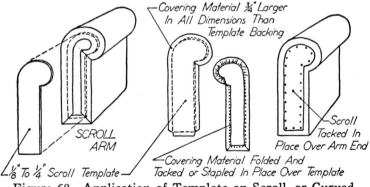

Figure 68—Application of Template on Scroll, or Curved Top Arm

stuffing and around the inside of the arm area. Then the muslin cover is tacked to the underside of the arm. The front is tacked in the curve on the front of the arm by the draw string method as described in Fig. 59. The templet (or template) is cut from heavy solid cardboard, thinly padded, then covered with only the final covering. It fits in place as shown in Fig. 68 and is "blind" tacked to the arm front, thus covering the tacking and folds made in forming the scroll covering.

Foam Rubber Padding For Arms—All cotton padding in arm upholstery can be substituted for by one-inch foam rubber. If the arm section in question must be filled out to make some particular shape such as the gently rounded flat top sofa arm, the underpadding or stuffing must be left as an element. The edge rolls must be filled correctly so that the foam rubber will blend into the edge to make a smooth surface. When there is not sufficient space to tack the glued on tacking strip to the top of the frame, wider tacking strips should be used. These can be pulled over the edge rolls and tacked on the underside.

Padded Top Arm Rest—The arm rest which has only the long horizontal member padded and covered, and the end "hand" pieces and vertical support members are of plain finished wood, is used for the most part in the "occasional" chair. This type of covering may be done at anytime before the back upholstery is applied. It is understuffed and padded all the way to the point where the arm fits into the back frame.

Chapter 9

PROJECT ELEMENTS—BACKS

Types of Backs

Without exception, all upholstery jobs will have some member of a back to consider, unless the project consists mainly of a stool or bench type piece. Whether the back is plain wood

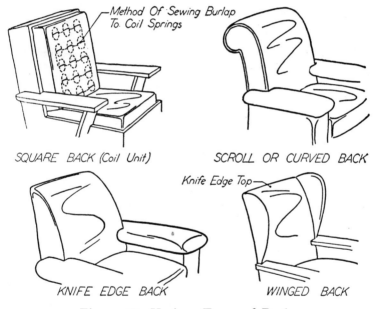

SQUARE BACK (Coil Unit)   SCROLL OR CURVED BACK

KNIFE EDGE BACK   WINGED BACK

Figure 69—Various Types of Backs

with no padding or covering or whether it is the extremely difficult overstuffed extra cushion affair, the consideration of its structure is a must in your planning. Among the different types of backs are the plain wood type (already mentioned), the separated and stuffed back (upholstery being only on a section above the seat), the webbed, with the webbed and coil spring unit, the sagless spring, and the solid base with foam rubber. The upholstery methods for these various units do not differ much with those for the seats, with the exception that the included spring units need not be quite so strong. Fig. 69 shows some of the various types of backs available to the upholsterer. Fig. 70 illustrates the development of two of these backs from the frame to the finished cover.

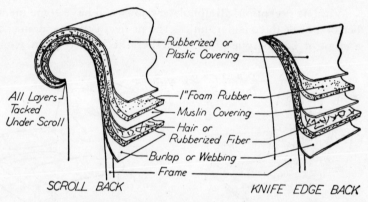

SCROLL BACK — Rubberized or Plastic Covering — 1"Foam Rubber — Muslin Covering — Hair or Rubberized Fiber — Burlap or Webbing — Frame — All Layers Tacked Under Scroll — KNIFE EDGE BACK

Figure 70—Process of Upholstering Scroll and
"Knife Edge" Back

Separated Backs—When the upper part of the chair back is to be upholstered it is seldom necessary to use any more than the simple webbing foundation with no springs of any sort. Padding, stuffing or foam rubber are sufficient over the jute webbing. If the back in question is to be completely covered, then it is necessary to stretch webbing on both sides of the frame. If the back in question is the picture frame type (as in older Victorian oval back chairs), then the front webbing can be excluded. The back webbing is the support webbing. The frame between is filled with padding and stuffing to the correct level and resiliency, then sewn in place and covered.

Webbed Support, Without Springs—In many cases the upholstery covers the entire length of the back, but still has no spring members as has the seat of the same unit. In this case, the webbing may be placed on the front of the frame and thinly stuffed and padded for a firm surface, as is prefer-able in simple straight back "occasional" chairs. If a more resilient back is preferred, then the support webbing can be placed on the back of the frame and the interior of the frame filled with fiber stuffing and padded out with cotton battons to the desired level. Here foam rubber may be substituted for the cotton padding. Since several grades of foam rubber are avail-able, the correct one should be chosen from the manufacturers directions. The muslin covering and the final cover are to be applied in the same manner as described in the section on seat covering.

Webbing and Coil Springs—In the case where the frame is too deep and a much more resilient back is desired the web-bing is applied to the back (see Figs. 43 and 48). The coil springs are laid out and tied or clipped in place with hog rings. The unit is now ready for the top covering or webbing and the final sewing of the coils in place. Apply the same methods described in the section on seats. Stuffing and padding can be of the standard rubberized fibers or hair and cotton. If foam rubber is desired, then the cotton padding is left off. The cov-ering for the back can consist of unimpregnated muslin covered by the final upholstery covering. Both are applied in the standard fashion as was described for seats.

Sagless Springs and Edge Wire Framing—When the sag-less spring is used, the frame must be strong enough to take the added stress, since little of the weight and strain is con-sumed in the webbing or the spring system. The forces are all transmitted to the frame sections. Reinforcement must be done in order to assure that the frame will not come apart in actual use. Refer to Figs. 28, 32 and 33 for the correct idea of frame supporting. If the frame is weak from dried glue joints or cracked members, then the joints should be cleaned and reglued before any reupholstery has been completed. As has been explained in the first chapter of this book, the sagless spring units used in the back sections are constructed in the same fashion as the seat units. However, less strong or slighter tensioned wire units (smaller diameter spring wire) are used. The application of edge wire is essentially the same as in the edge wire on seat structures. The use of torsion springs (see Fig. 6) in the corners is advised and also the application of edge springs, to maintain the position of the edge wire, as is shown in Fig. 5 for the seat sections. In many cases the seat section can be equipped with the sagless spring and the back equipped with coil springs and ordinary webbing. Since the back does not usually have to support the weight the seat does, ordinary construction will serve as well and will require no frame bracing. The sagless spring construction has been shown in Figs. 1 through 6 in the first chapter.

Covering and Padding of Sagless Springs—Sagless springs must be covered with some form of insulator and may be fibre stuffed and padded with cotton or foam rubber.

Solid Base and Foam Rubber Padding (Solid and Cored Stock)—On many simple bench types (similar to auto seats with no arms) the simplest and quickest upholstery method utilizes the solid plywood base (¾" thick) and either built up foam rubber or thicker cored stock units (see Fig. 12). The base and frame must be the correct depth so the foam rubber will stick at least 3 to 4 inches above the edge of the frame. If the complete unit is to be covered, the frame and solid base board must be level and the cored stock slightly larger than the area of the base—about 1" on either side. With this surplus, the foam rubber can be pulled tight in place, forming a well made back support. The canvas or heavy muslin undercovering will hold the rubber unit in tension. If the plain solid wooden base is first painted and then covered with rubberized fiber or hair, then with foam rubber over that, it makes an easy unit to cover with canvas or heavy muslin undercovering. The chapter on seats has given a full account of this method of covering and upholstering.

In some cases, when planning to upholster the backs of seats or benches, the solid board backing can have coil springs tacked or stapled in place and the top of the coil springs webbed and tied, as in the fashion of ordinary webbed seats. Then the whole spring unit is overstuffed with hair or fiber, padded with foam rubber and covered with muslin or canvas. The thicker the underpadding and the foam rubber unit, the more resilient the back area. It is necessary to drill ventilation holes about 4" apart, and about 1" in diameter. These holes give the foam rubber a chance to dry out and to keep the unit from collecting a stale odor. Backs of furniture cushioned or upholstered with foam rubber need not be covered with a moisture proof cloth or plastic.

Top Padding (Curved and Rounded)—The tops of most backs have some treatment or other which includes extra padding. In those cases where the arms have a knife edge and a

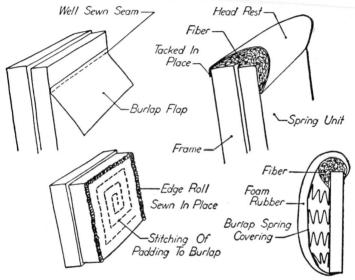

Figure 71—Application of Top Padding on Backs

similar top on the back is desired, this total effect can be realized only through the use of extra padding. With the scroll, curved or round top, or the knife edge, the preparation is the same. The back frame must be webbed sprung with the burlap covering placed over the springs before the top padding can be added. A strip of burlap or canvas is sewn to the spring cover (Fig. 71) at the top, then drawn up over the hair or fibre padding and fastened in the back of the roll. The shape of the underpadding must be taken into consideration as the unit is formed. Lumps and depressions must be smoothed out with the upholsterer's regulator (looks like a cooking skewer). The ends then can be folded in and tacked down so as to produce a

smooth side which can be covered by the muslin covering and
the final covering. Strips of foam rubber can be made to conform to the desired shape by tightly pulling the covering strip
of cloth. The rubberized fibre or hair must be tacked in place
at various spots to keep it from shifting out of place after the
piece has been put in service. When covering the top roll, take
into consideration the other edge rolls which might run up
the sides of the back and into a point where a smooth joint
must be made with the top padding. If the unit is so constructed, then the covering of the top roll must take place at
the same time as the edge rolls. After the burlap covering has
been added over the understuffing of the whole back, the over-
padding and stuffing can be added and covered.

Wing and Upper Arm Sections—Older pieces of overstuffed
furniture have wing sections which have been discussed par-
tially in a previous chapter. The type of upholstery which is
to be used on these sections must be considered before the back
itself is begun. In many cases the wing must be upholstered
first, and in others its edging or understuffing must be affixed
at the same time. This insures a smooth integrated job of the
joining of the two members. Seldom do the units call for any
type of springs at all. You do have a choice as to whether the
webbing is placed on the back of the wing with the center of
the frame filled with stuffing and padding to give a more
resilient surface, or placed on the front to give simply a padded surface which does not add to the complication of the
unit. In any case the wing or arm unit, when finished, must
not only look as a part of the back but must be strong enough
to withstand some stress and strain. The padding must be
sufficient to bow out the surface to cover the joining crack
between the two sections, the wings and the back.

Stuffing Separate Cushions—One of the most difficult jobs
in any upholstery project is the stuffing of separate cushions
either with hair stuffing, Marshall units or foam rubber. In the
professional job, the stuffing is layed out in a clamping machine and the sewed cover is inserted like a bag over the flat
iron side of the machine. The handle is turned and into the
cushion case is stuffed the innards of whatever sort is desired.
If cushions are involved in your upholstery project, you might

conceivably have a professional upholsterer do the stuffing. However, it is possible either to sew the case top in place when the stuffing has been layed in place or to build some stuffing iron tins yourself. These tins are made out of sheet metal (galvanized iron). They fit together encasing the stuffing and slide as a unit inside the cushion case. When the irons are with-

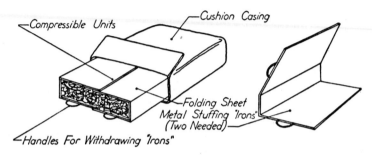

Figure 72—Stuffing "Irons" Used for Stuffing Cushions

drawn one at a time, the stuffing is left in place inside the case (see Fig. 72). With the small upholsterer's pins the cloth front of the cushion can be pinned in place and hand stitched.

Marshall Units for Cushions—These bagged spring units are somewhat easier to install in cushions for overstuffed furniture. They should be layed out and sewed together to fit the shape of the final cushion leaving room for the two layers of padding cotton which must go on all sides of the units. The cotton can be gently stitched in place and the different pieces of the cushion surface can be pinned in place. When the full unit is covered, then the final stitching can take place. It is not suggested that cushions be stuffed, as it were, by the handfuls with raw cotton, as would a down pillow or a paper sack. Lumps and dips must be avoided at all costs. The final judgment of your project will come from those who have to sit on it.

Chapter 10

METAL FRAME FURNITURE

Earlier in the text I mentioned that more explanation was to come concerning those elements of interior and exterior furniture which were upholstered with either a single slung layer or a webbing of canvas or plastic cloth. The modern trend toward tubular metal, reinforced plastic and bare frame furniture has required a simpler form of upholstery or covering. This section of the text will cover those processes necessary for the replacement of these various types of single layer or webbed upholstery. The last part of this section will cover the new type of furniture construction where resin impregnated fiberglass is used as the major frame sections. In this type of construction the especially strong plastic is molded in self supporting shells and fit together to form the chair or sofa or whatever. In most cases the spring supports (sagless springs), webbing, padding and felting and upholstery is done the same way as in conventional furniture. However, where straight smooth arm sides and back areas are required, the final upholstery is glued and rolled in place and must be specially treated in removal for re-upholstery.

Outdoor Furniture — Those pieces of furniture which are exposed to the elements will, of course need re-upholstery more often than those used in the interior of the home. Outdoor or yard furniture is made primarily of metal: iron, tubular steel, aluminum, and more recently of magnesium tubing. The average priced unit (lawn chair, lounge, deck swing, etc.) is of metal; and within that price class the lighter metals are used in the better units. They are strong enough and light enough for the lady of the house to move herself, but they pose a problem of metal repair and more often a problem in replacement of the cloth or plastic seat and back elements. Considering the various types of metals and their form and finally the method of construction I will list each type of metal frame (tubular, solid, etc.) and of what metals it is most likely to be made.

Solid black iron of small diameter

    Most usual construction: Welded............................permanent

    Alternate constructions: Riveted..........................permanent

       Bolted ....demountable

       Wrench-tightened couplings ....demountable

Hollow Tubular Steel (¾″ diameter at least)

    Most usual construction: Spot welded................permanent

    Alternate constructions: Spot welded or

      indented couplings ....permanent

      Riveted ....permanent

      Bolted ....demountable

Hollow Tubular Aluminum (¾″ diameter at least)

    Most usual construction:

      Bolted (self assembled type)........................demountable

    Alternate constructions: Spot welded or

      indented couplings ....permanent

      Cold welded...permanent

      Riveted ....permanent

Hollow Tubular Magnesium (¾″ diameter at least)

    Most usual construction:

      Bolted (self assembled type)........................demountable

      Force fit (cold weld) coupling or

        swedged fit ends.......................................permanent

    Alternate constructions: Riveted........................permanent

Structural Metal ("I" beam shape or channel iron shape, etc.)

    Most usual construction: Welded for iron, and steel

      Spot welded for aluminum

      Bolted or riveted for magnesium

Wood and Iron or Other Metal Combined

    Most usual construction:

      Bolted or lag screws.....................................demountable

Tubular or Structural resin-fiberglass with or without metal

    Most usual construction: Formed in molding of plastic

      and bonded...permanent

    With metal frame: Bolted...................................demountable

Wood without any metal

    Most usual construction: Bolted........................demountable

Rivets ....permanent
Wood screws ....demountable
Alternate constructions: Glued....................................permanent
Pegged ....permanent
(Wedge pegged) ....demountable

Indoor furniture — For the most part interior furniture is constructed along the same lines as those already explained but the strict requirements for craftsmanship in interior furniture almost dictates that some form of welding be used so that the joints may be smooth ground at the factory. Hence, those coverings that are of the single layer variety are either sewn in place or are of the type that have support pockets sewn in the canvas which engage the metal chair frame making a sort of sling. Seldom are they of the type, so common in yard or garden furniture, that has loops sewn in the canvas at either end of the piece and is slipped in place before the chair or lounge is assembled and bolted, riveted, or welded into a solid construction.

Commercial or office furniture is often a combination of wooden frames with tubular steel or aluminum arms and legs. In most cases these added metal sections are bolted in place before the springs are covered. This type of re-upholstery job has been explained in the sections on upholstery for seats, backs, etc. of conventional furniture.

Kitchen or dinette furniture is in most instances composed of formed metal legs and arms of tubular steel with a seat or back board cut for the correct size of the unit. It is simply padded as explained in the section on chair seats and backs and then covered with the final fabric. The metal arms and legs are screwed in place after the back is recovered or repaired.

Metal-legged bar stools, which are often used in the recreation room, have detachable seats which can be upholstered or covered separately and then re-bolted in place on the tubular metal legs.

Replacement of natural or synthetic fabric — As you look over the chart which shows the type and methods of outdoor and indoor metal furniture construction you will see that there are essentially two types of frame work: that which can be demounted, i.e. dis-assembled prior to the installation of new seating and backing fabrics, and that which is of a permanently constructed nature which has had the fabric elements either sewn in place, or sewn prior to construction and slipped in place before the unit was welded, or riveted permanently. A new type of application of fabrics, especially for the 2″ to 4″ wide plastic webbing, or the conventional canvas or burlap webbing, involves a series of ⅛″ holes on the inner side of the tubular steel frame. The strips of webbing are cut sufficiently long to wrap around the outside of the tubular frame then underneath and up to the inner side where the remaining two inches of webbing is wrapped around a special metal cleat (this cleat is as wide as the webbing and curved to fit snugly on the surface of the tubular frame for about 1″ of its circumference). After the one end of the webbing is around the tubular frame (over and around the outside, underneath and up to the inside, and around the cleat) a split rivet is pushed through the hole in the cleat, and into the corresponding hole in the frame. Being a spring-type rivet it holds the cleat in place and thus the ends of the webbing. The second end of the webbing is fastened in place tightly with the aid of a webbing stretcher as shown in figure 15 earlier in the text. Special care should be taken to use only the best heavy grade of canvas or jute-burlap natural fiber webbing, or in the case of plastic webbing, one which has enough tension strength not to stretch out of shape. Saran, Fiber glass in Saran plastic and plastic impregnated natural fibers are but a few such types. In replacing the webbing which has interwoven webs across the frame (the long webbing strips running from the top of the back to the foot of the seat) the short webbing strips should be installed first, and the longer ones last.

Sewn Loops or Snap Buttoned Loops — The sewn loops (sewn in place by hand using the sailmakers stitch and having a secure knot at either end of the waxed sewing twine) or the snap button loops (which can be installed with the aid of a small tool and a kit of various snap buttons—both obtainable at the dry goods store) can be used with the permanent or demountable types of construction. It is best to get a non-rusting variety of snap buttons which are also large enough

to support the weight of a grown person. In proceeding with
either of these two types of webbing or sheet replacement you
should gauge the size of each different piece you will need
from the old material or fabric which has been removed. In
the case of webbing, you can use the sewn loop for either
natural or synthetic plastic webbing but the snap buttons are
not advised for plastic webs. Either method can be used
when you are replacing wider widths of seating or backing.
In the case of wide canvas or cloth units it is best to hem the
cloth on a sewing machine after cutting to the correct width.
Then when the correct lengths are found the pieces can be cut
to size. The hem will prevent raveling of the edge, and a
messy job. The work, of course, will be started from one side.
Since in most cases it will be difficult to obtain sufficient tension of the cross piece, here are some suggestions for increas-
ing the tension and still providing room to sew the final loop.
Finish one loop over whichever side of tubular rail you wish,
leaving the full length of all the wide cloth hemmed strip you
will need. After the first loop is sewn in place, wrap the long
end of the remaining strip over the top of and down and underneath the other rail, just as if you were going to sew it in
place; but instead carry it across underneath, up and around
to the top side again. In this manner you can pull it tight and
pin it in place over the middle of the distance between the two
side rails. Simply fold back the long end away from where
you will sew the second loop in place. After the loop around
the second side rail is sewn, unpin the long strip, fold back and
cut off, leaving about 1" of cloth before the stitching. Another
method is to tension the sides of the tubular rails with clothesline or furniture clamps causing them to be closer together by
at least ½", but care should be taken not to shorten the distance between by too much.

Snap buttons, should be applied to the correct webbing
which has been "turned over" i.e. hemmed at the end to keep
the fabric from coming loose. The same thing should be done
on all four sides of wider seat or back members. If careful
measurements are taken, the snaps applied to the webbing or
canvas at the work bench will fit when applied to the tubular
frame of the unit of furniture. If the snaps will not close easily,

then the frame may be tensioned in by the use of a bar clamp or clothesrope. When all the snaps are in place the tension may be released.

Demountable Metal Frames — If it is possible to easily disassemble the frame of any type of metal furniture so that machine sewn loops can be slipped into place, I would suggest this type of procedure. The strength and neatness of machine stitching can not be denied. Often in this case it is wise to use a double thickness of seating material or canvas since the added strength will increase the life of the fibers outdoors. In all these cases it is wise to use the old cloth, webbing, or strip material as a general pattern. Adaptions can be made as you see fit. Do not use inexpensive canvas, webbing or plastics or the job will soon have to be done over. The weather is tough on natural fibers but much tougher on those fibers which are strained and torn by being over loaded.

Canvas and Leather Sling Type of Covering — There is little that can be said about the replacement of this type of covering, except that the key to its replacement lies in two things: good material, and accurate following of the old covering as to size, the cut of the cloth, and the method and places of sewing. The original manufacturer may have used cheap material but chances are he cut the material in the best way to get maximum strength out of what he did use. Follow his example, in the cutting and sewing only.

I mentioned a new type of plastic furniture frame which takes the place of the conventional wood frame. This frame is made of resin impregnated glass fibers, molded into a strong shape under tons of pressure and intense heat. Each section, the back, the sides, the arms are made separately and then bonded, or mechanically fastened together. The upholstery is sprung and covered in the same fashion as most modern furniture but where there is a flat side, back or other area which does not need padding for comfort, this area is covered with the final upholstery fabric glued in place and rolled out smooth. In order to replace these areas of covering the glue must be removed much in the manner of wallpaper and new cloth re-applied.

INDEX

Preface.

THE Puritan is not a soldier by choice, quite the contrary; he has the strongest aversion to bloody-minded men, and would desire as earnestly as ever Gladstone did to be delivered from blood-guiltiness; but when King Charles I. left no other door open, the Puritan went boldly through in the fear of God and for justice as between man and man.

But many of these men, nay, most of them, had what we now call the 'Nonconformist conscience,' and that had to be dealt with, soothed, satisfied, convinced, justified.

This was the work of the 'Souldier's Catechisme,' and I think it will be admitted that it was work admirably done, and exactly suited to the men it was meant for. It was not written above their heads, as so many a learned treatise on the King's supremacy; it was not in the language of Babylon, which their soul abhorred, but it was the language of Zion, which they had learned and loved from childhood.

In the great Civil War the Press was a very powerful instrument, the advantage strongly lying on the side of the Roundhead Party, as their pamphleteers were of the people, and wrote so as to be 'understanded of the people.' Two instances will make this clear. In 1643, just before the 'Souldier's Catechisme' was issued to the army, there appeared

the

the ' *Rebell's Catechism,*' *composed in an easy and familiar way, to let them see the heinousness of their offence, the weakness of their strongest subterfuges, and to recall them to their duties both to God and man. It was a quarto, much too big for any rebel's pocket, and the way it tried to recall them to their duties can be judged by some of the marginal references, viz., V. Stanford's Pleas, cap. 2; Coke on Littleton, l. 2, c. 11, § 200; Stat. 25, Ed. 3, cap. 2; Eucher. Lugdunens, et alii; Bract., l. 1, c. 3, § 4, etc. The book (penes me) is anonymous, but is attributed to Peter Heylin, D.D., a well-known Royalist controversialist. What rebel, I wonder, would look at it twice, even for curiosity?*

Next year (1644) *there appeared on the Puritan side* ' *The Cavalier's New Common Prayer unclasp't.*' *This bitterly sarcastic and amusing production (penes me) with a strong spice of seeming Puritanic irreverence, must have made many a Roundhead give way to laughter ' holding both his sides.' This is a rare pamphlet, fetching £3 18s. at Sotheby's in 1897. Being 4to. size, it is occasionally found bound up with other pamphlets, and thus copies have been preserved; binding is often the only chance of salvation a pamphlet has; and possibly the uncommonly small size of the ' Souldier's Catechisme' and the character of the people who carried it on their persons will account for there being only two known. For these Puritans were not bibliophiles, although they were given to bibliolatry, and would no more have thought of binding their soldiers' guides than we should think of binding our Bradshaws.*

However,

However, the point is that the Roundheads were by far the shrewdest combatants in this paper war, and the present little book was one of their most effective weapons.

Like the Maccabees of old, the Puritan warriors of Cromwell's time had the sword in their hand and the praises of God in their mouth. In their forced marches and rapid movements they could not be burdened with many impedimenta, but there would be room under the commonest soldier's leathern jacket for his little Pocket Bible and Catechism which had been composed for him and had received the ' imprimatur ' of the Parliamentary censors.

The literature specially designed for soldiers is very limited both in amount and variety. This is just what we should naturally expect. A soldier on active service was supposed to have something more important to do than to read. If not too tired he might fight his battles o'er again round the camp fire, he might argue, discuss, approve, or object, but a solitary reader would be scouted, unless his book were a spiritual guide to strengthen him in the fight, i.e., God's Word, or something strictly founded on it. But, shortly after the election of the Long Parliament, and especially in the years 1642-4, it began to be clear to all who had any foresight that the common soldiers were the persons who would have to be reckoned with eventually, so pamphlets or rather tracts, as we should call them, began to be issued for the soldier's religious and political edification. They have most of them quite disappeared, though a stray copy may be found here and there in our great libraries. One such is ' The Christian Souldier; or Preparation for Battaile,
A Legend

A Legend containing true rules for a Souldier, in whom at once is met Religion and Resolution.' Published by a well-wisher to the Gown and Sword, T. J., 1642, in 4to. This is Royalist in tendency. Not one seems to be issued by the authorities except the ' Souldier's Catechisme.'

It should never be forgotten, most of all in this material semi-pagan age in which we live, or to which we are apparently drifting, that Puritanism is a permanent element in human nature. One might even say, in spite of its frequent exaggerated forms, that it is one of the strongest, noblest and most valuable elements that help to build up the ordinary citizen. It is of this stuff that great and enduring nations are made. It is this sober, serious, honest, religious frame of mind that has so greatly helped to make both England and New England the great countries they now are. A sense of justice and right living combined with a serious view of life would form its chief characteristics. Privilege and tyranny are the object of its bitterest hate, more especially in things spiritual.

Its influence has been mostly of the silent sort. Not much chronicled in the records of the court, the castle, or the camp ; an alien, as a rule, to the great conquerors, diplomats and historic personages who fill up the roll of fame, but chiefly dwelling in the homes and the hearts of humbler men of whom the world hears little.

There have been exceptions, when ' the hour ' has brought forth ' the man,' and typical of these are such men as Cromwell and Judas Maccabeus—patriots and soldiers and puritans ' par excellence.'

The

Preface.

The author of this little book is unknown. It was most probably written to order at the suggestion of the chiefs of the Puritan Party connected with the Parliament's army, where now Cromwell was a rising and leading commander. It was evidently meant to be a companion to what is known as Cromwell's Pocket Bible of the year before (1643). Books written to order were by no means unusual with the Puritan Party. Milton's ' Eikonoklastes,' and his ' Pro Populo Anglicano Defensio,' were both written at the express command of Cromwell and the other leaders in the Council of State.

It has been said with a great degree of truth that if Eikon Basilike ' had been issued only a few weeks earlier, it would have kept the King's head on his shoulders. It is an equally just observation that this little ' vade mecum ' for the Roundhead soldiers helped considerably to catechise the King's head ' off ' his shoulders, for if it had not been for the strong feeling in the predominant portion of the army, fostered by such a skilfully-worded religious primer as this Soldier's Catechism is, the chiefs of the Republican Party would never have dared to ' slay the Lord's anointed ' openly in the presence of thousands of his subjects.

As I stated in the prospectus, this literary curiosity has been practically unknown for more than 300 years. No historians, delighting in local colour, have ever brought this little book on the scene, for the good reason that they did not know of its existence. Only one notice of it has come to my knowledge, and that was more than 200 years ago—viz., in 1684—when a certain John Turner, referring to Charles II
and

and the Soldier's Catechism, writes: ' It was without ques-
tion none of the meanest instruments in bringing his royal
father to the block.'
How strange that a printed historical document,

> *' Big with the fate ' of King and State,*
> *Should thus be brought to light so late !*

I offer this fac-simile of one of the rarities of my library
to the consideration of the historical student and the general
public, ending this brief preface on the day when the news-
papers have scattered far and wide the patriotic Chatham
speech of Lord Rosebery, himself eulogist and admirer of
our Cromwell. In it he tells Englishmen everywhere that
they are in the midst of ' the most formidable war ' our
country has ever engaged in, a war rendered still more
formidable by the unanimous opinion of all Europe being
arrayed against us.

He bids us, however, not fear for the issue, and with the
quiet steady confidence of a veteran Ironside, adds this
cheering remark, ' They have not got to the bottom of Old
England's resources yet.'

If we cherish the serious God-fearing resolution of
Cromwell's ' Souldiers ' they never will. So may it be.

WALTER BEGLEY.

HAMPSTEAD, *January* 24, 1900.

THE
SOULDIERS

CATECHISME:

Compoſed for

The Parliaments Army:

Conſiſting of two Parts : wherein
are chiefly taught :

1 *The Iuſtification*
2 *The Qualification* } *of our Souldiers.*

Written for the Incouragement and In-
ſtruction of all that have taken up Armes in
this Cauſe of God and his People; eſpe-
cially the common Souldiers.

---

2 Sam. 10. 12. *Be of good courage, and let us
play the men for our people, and for the Ci-
ties of our God, and the Lord do that which
ſeemeth him good.*

Deut. 23. 9. *When the Hoſt goeth forth againſt
thine enemies, then keepe thee from every
wicked thing.*

Imprimatur. JA. CRANFORD.

Printed for J. Wright *in the* Old-Baily. 1644

THE
SOULDIERS
CATECHISME:

Compoſed for the Parliaments Armie.

Queſtion.

Hat Profeſſion are you of?

Anſwer. I am a Chriſtian and a ſouldier.

Q. Is it lawfull for Chriſtians to be ſouldiers?

A. Yea doubtleſſe : we have Arguments enough to warrant it.

1. God calls himſelf a man of war, and Lord of Hoſts.

2. *Abraham* had a Regiment of 318. Trained men.

3. *David* was imployed in fighting the Lords battels.

4. The Holy Ghoſt makes honourable mention of *Davids* Worthies.

A 2   5. God

5 God himselfe taught *David* to fight.

6. The noble gift of valour is given for this purpose.

7. The New Testament mentioneth two famous Centurions.

8. The Bap ist doth not require the souldiers to leave their profession, *Luke* 3.14.

9. Many comparisons are taken from this Calling in the New Testament.

10. There have been many famous Martyrs of this profession.

Q. What does our Saviour meane then by those words? Mat. 5. 39.

A. 1. Christ there onely forbids private revenge and resistance.

2. Scripture is the best interpreter of Scripture : we know that other places of Scripture do warrant taking up of Arms in some cases.

Q. What side are you of, and for whom doe you fight?

A. I am for King and Parliament : or, in plainer termes ;

1. I fght to recover the King out of the hands of a Popish Malignant Company, that have seduced His Majesty with their wicked Counsels, and have withdrawne him from his Parliament.

2. I fight for the Lawes and Liberties of my Countrey, which are now in danger to be overthrowne by them that have long laboured to

bring

bring into this Kingdome an Arbitrary, and Tyrannicall Government.

3. I fight for the prefervation of our Parliament, in the being whereof (under God) confifts the glory and welfare of this Kingdome; if this Foundation be overthrown, we fhall foone bee the moft flavifh Nation in the Chriftian World.

4. I fight in the defence and maintenance of the true Proteftant Religion, which is now violently oppofed, and will be utterly fuppreft in this Kingdome; and the Popifh Religion again advanced, if the Armies raifed againft the Parliament prevaile.

Q. *But is it not againft the King that you fight in this Caufe?*

A. No furely: yet many do abufe the world with this bafe and abfurd objection: our onely aime is,

1. To refcue the King out of the hands of his and the Kingdomes enemies; and to maintaine his Honour and juft Prerogatives.

2. We endeavour to defend that which the King is bound to defend, both by his Oath and Office.

3. Wee take up Armes againft the enemies of Jefus Chrift, who in His Majefties name make warre againft the Church and People of God.

4. If the King will joine himself with them that seek the ruine of his people, and the overthrow of Religion, surely both we and all good Subjects, may lawfully stand in the defence of both; as the people did against King *Saul* in the case of *Ionathan*, 1 *King.* 14. 45.

5. We do no more then what our Brethren of Scotland did, when they came into this Kingdome with an Army some three or foure yeares since; whose Action the King and both Houses have cleered from all Rebellion, and they remaine justified in what they then did, to all posterity, by an Act of Parliament.

Q. Hath not the King published many Protestations that he will maintain our Lawes, Liberties and Religion? why then do we feare the subversion of them?

A. 1. Many things have been published in his Majesties name, which in all probability he never saw or knew of.

2. Though the King himselfe may intend really and well, yet the Sonnes of *Zervia* are too strong for him.

3. It is not to be imagined that a Popish Army will defend the Protestant Religion, or lawlesse Libertines, the Lawes of the Land.

4. We find by wofull experience that he hath many waies failed in divers of those large Promises and Protestations, notwithstanding that

God hath been fo often called to witneffe.

5. They fay it is a *Maxime* now at Court, that Faith is not to be kept with Hereticks, and fuch, doe fome there, account all true Proteftants.

Q. *How can you that are Souldiers for the Parliament anfwer that place of Paul,* Rom. 13. 1,2,3. &c.

A. 1. That place requires not obedience to any unlawfull Commands, neither doth any other place of Scripture, we are no further to obey man, then may ftand with the will of God.

2. They are grofly miftaken which fay the King is the higheft power; Indeed he is the higheft perfon in his Dominions, but the Lawes and Courts of the Kingdom are above him in power, and the King himfelf is limited and fubject to the meaneft Court in the Land : Therefore furely the high Court of Parliament muft needs be the higher Power, which not to obey, is to refift the Ordinance of God.

3. Suppofe the King were the Higher Power, yet if he fhall intend or permit the ruine o his Subjects, both nature and grace allowes people to preferve themfelves.

4. If the King be the higheft power by conftitution, yet is his power now in other hands by ufurpation. The Queen, *Iermin, Briftol, Digby, Cottington, Windebanke, Porter,* and many others

A 4   thers

thers, have for a long time, and do still mannage the greatest affaires of the Kingdome; so that it were a miserable thing to be subjected in conscience (as that Text imports, if some mens exposition might passe for orthodox Divinity) to such enemies and incendiaries both of Church and Commonwealth.

Q. What is it that moves you to take up Arms, and to ingage your selfe in this Civill Warre?

A. 1. The love I beare to my Countrey.

2. The preservation of our Parliament, Laws and Liberties.

3. The defence of our Religion against Poperie.

4. The care of our Posterity.

5. The generall forwardnesse of all good people.

6. The consent, and provocation of ull Gods Ministers.

7. The command of the Parliament, which is the Higher Power.

8. The necessity that now lies upon all that feare God in the Land.

Q. What do you think then of those Protestants which sit still, and do not put forth themselves in these times?

A. 1. Either they are not convinced of the necessity.

2. Or they are but luke-warme Professors.

3. Or

3. Or they are of bafe and private fpirits.

4. Or they are faint-hearted cowards.

5. Or they are fecret enemies to God and his Caufe.

Q. *What danger are fuch Newters in?*

A. 1. God takes fpeciall notice of their difpofition and carriage, and will deale with them accordingly.

2. In Gods account all fuch are enemies; they that are not with him are againft him.

3. They deferve neither refpect nor protection from Church or Commonwealth.

4. They are in danger to be fpued out of Chrifts mouth, *Rev.*3.16.

5. They are directly under that dreadful curfe which the Angell of the Lord denounced againft *Merofh*, Judg.5.23.

Q. *What fay you then of thofe Proteftants, which fight on the other fide, and joyne with the Enemies of our Religion, Parliament, and Countrey?*

A. 1. I fay, that they are unworthy the name of Proteftants.

2. I fay, that they maintain the caufe of Antichrift.

3. That they are the fhame and blemifhes of Religion.

4. That none of their weapons fhall profper, *Ifa.*54.17.

5. That

5. That God will utterly undoe them, *Zeph.* 3.19.

6 That their fwords fhall enter into their owne hearts, *Pfal.*37.15.

7. That all the blood that hath been fhed lies upon their fcore.

8. That they are in the high-way to perdition, without repentance.

Q. *What is the reafon thinke you, that fo many Proteftants, of all degrees, joyne with our Papifb enemies?*

A. 1. Many are onely Proteftants in name, but indeed are Papifts, or Atheifts in heart.

2. Many are drawne in to joyn with that Party out of a bafe feare of fuffering in their eftates, fuppofing the Kings fide would be the fafeft.

3. Many to avoid the Juftice of Parliament, have hazarded the ruine of their Countrey, to fave themfelves from their deferved punifhment.

4. Many have ingaged themfelves with the Kings Party, in hope to make up their broken fortunes.

5. Many for feare of Reformation, which they are not able to indure, and therefore joyne with them that oppofe it.

6. Many out of a defperate fpirit of Malignancy, and an implacable enmity againft the people
ple

ple of God, and all goodneſſe.

Q. What is it that you chiefly aime at in this Warre?

A. 1. At the pulling down of Babylon, and rewarding her as ſhe hath ſerved us, *Pſal.* 137. 8

2. At the ſuppreſſion of an Antichriſtian Prelacy, conſiſting of Archbiſhops, Biſhops, &c.

3. At the Reformation of a moſt corrupt, lazie, infamous, ſuperſtitious, ſoule-murdering Clergie.

4. At the advancement of Chriſts Kingdome and the purity of his Ordinances.

5. At the bringing to Juſtice the enemies of our Church and State.

6. At the regulating of our Courts of Juſtice, which have been made the ſeats of iniquity and unrighteouſneſſe.

7. At the upholding of our Parliaments, which are the Subjeꞇts beſt Inheritance, and the Crowne of our Nation.

8. At the preſervation, and continuing of the Goſpell to our poſterity, and the generations to come.

Q. What hopes have you of prevailing in this Cauſe?

A. We have incouragements enough to aſſure us of good ſucceſſe: there be many arguments to confirm our hope.

1. From the juſtneſſe and goodneſſe of the Cauſe.　　　　　　　　　　　2. From

2. From the courfe that hath been taken.

3. From the condition of thofe that are ingaged in the bufineffe.

4. From the quality of our enemies.

5. From the cheerfullneffe of moft mens fpirits in this Action.

6. From the many defeats and victories al ready given and obtained.

7. From the affiftance of our Brethren of Scotland.

8. From the Covenant which all the well-affected of the Kingdome have entred into.

Q. Explaine thefe more particularly and in order, and firft fhew me what hopes you conceive from the goodneffe of the Caufe?

A. 1. A good Caufe puts life and courage into mens hearts.

2. A good Caufe hath GOD ever fiding with it.

3. A good Caufe daunts and difmays the adverfe party.

4. A good Caufe will undoubtedly prevaile at laft.

Q. What is your incouragement from the courfe that hath been taken?

A. 1. In that all faire and Chriftian waies have been attempted before wee tooke up Armes.

2. In that the Lord was folemnly and generally

nerally fought unto before this bufineffe was undertaken.

3. In that it was undertaken with good advice, and is guided by a multitude of Counfellors.

4. In that it is ftill followed with the Prayers and humiliations of all the faithfull in the Land.

Q. *What hope have you from them that are ingaged in this Warre?*

A. 1. Becaufe all the faithfull and godly Minifters of the Kingdome, do fide with us in this Caufe.

2. Becaufe the moft of our Commanders are men of dif-ingaged and Publique Spirits.

3. Becaufe our men generally are fo full of courage and refolution.

4. Becaufe we have fo many godly and religious Souldiers in our Armies.

Q. *What from the quality of your enemies?*

A. Wee may conclude that God will not profper them.

1. Becaufe they are for the moft part Papifts and Atheifts, with whom we have to deale.

2. Becaufe they are generally the moft horrible Curfers and Plafphemers in the World.

3. Becaufe

3. Becaufe they are, for the moft part, inhu-
mane, barbarous and cruell.

4. Becaufe they are enemies to God, and the
power of goodneffe, and therefore the Lord will
fcatter them.

Q. *What doe you gather from the cheerfulneffe*
of their fpirits, that are of your party?

A. 1. 'Tis an Argument that God hath rai
fed his fervants to do fome great worke, *Pfal.*
149. 5. 9.

2. 'Tis an Argument that God will profper
thofe whom he hath made fo willing, *Judg.* 5. 2.

3. 'Tis an Argument that fuch as are fo willing and cheerfull in this bufineffe, will goe on
couragioufly.

4. 'Tis an Argument that they are fo well
affured of the goodneffe of their Caufe, that they
will live and die in it.

Q. *What doe you conclude from the good fuc-*
ceffe that your fide hath already had?

A. 1. That Almighty God declares himfelfe
a friend to our Party.

2. That he hath already much abated the courage of our enemies.

3. That we have all the reafon in the World
to truft God for the future, who hath done fo
much for us.

4. That the Lord will glorifie himfelf more
and more in his Churches behalf.

Q. *What*

Q. *What hopes have you from your Brethren of Scotland ?*

A. 1. We have cause to acknowledge Gods great mercy in bringing them to our assistance es this time.

2. Their numbers and preparations are great, and they a couragious and warlike Nation.

3. They have given sufficient testimony of late of their love and faithfullnesse towards our Nation.

4. They are as much concerned in this Quarrell as wee, and are resolved to joine with us in it.

Q. *But what grounds have you to comfort your selves from the National Covenant, which you say so many have entred into ?*

A. 1. Because it is a testimony of our generall humiliation, and a good beginning of Reformation.

2. Because it is the joy and desire of all good Christians throughout the Land.

3. Because Popery never received so deadly a blow in this Kingdome, as by this Covenant.

4. Because all the Parliaments affaires have prospered well since the Covenant was taken, witnesse our many victories and successes : As 1. Glocester, 2. Newbury, 3. Winchby, neere Horne-Castle, 4. Hull, the same day, 5. Lincolne.

colns, 6. Gainsborough, 7. Arundell Castle, 8.
Nantwich, 9. Alsford near Winchester, besides
many other defeats given the enemy. and divers
other places of lesser note recovered, without a-
ny considerable losse on our side.

Q. *But is it not a lamentable thing that Christians of the same Nation, should thus imbrue
their hands in one anothers blood?*

A. I confesse it is : But as the case now
stands, there is an inevitable and absolute necessity of fighting laid upon the good people of the
Land.

1. Is it not high time to stand upon our guard,
when our enemies have drawn their Swords upon us, to invade our persons, and whatsoever is
dear to us.

2. God now calls upon us to avenge the
blood of his Saints that hath been shed in the
Land, and those many outrages which have been
committed against his servants.

3. The whole Church of God calls upon us
to come in to the help of the Lord and his people against the mighty.

4. Our children and posterity call upon us to
maintain those Liberties, and that Gospel, which
we received from our fore-fathers.

5. We are not now to look at our enemies as
Country-men or Irishmen, or fellow-Prote-
stants, but as the enemies of God and our Religion,

gion, and fiders with Antichrift ; and fo our eye is not to pitie them, nor our fword to fpare them, *Ier.*48.10.

Q. *There are a great many on the Kings Party that have beene held honeft men, &c. will your fword make no difference betweene them and others?*

A. 1. If they joyn themfelves with the malignant Party, we cannot know them from Malignants.

2. It is to be feared, that fuch were never of us, becaufe they are fo cruell againft us : hypocrites commonly when they are unmaskt, prove the moft dangerous enemies.

Q. *Who do you thinke were the Authors, and occafioners of this unnaturall Warre?*

A. 1. The Jefuites, thofe fire-brands of mifchiefe, with all the Popifh party.

2. The Bifhops, and the rotten Clergie, with all the Prelaticall party.

3. The Delinquents, that were not able to abide the triall of Juftice, with all the Malignant party.

4. The formall Gofpellers of the Kingdome, that hate a Reformation, with all the Atheiftiall party.

Q. *Do not many of them that you count your enemies, ftand for Religion as well as you?*

A. 1. Surely they are mad, that thinke the

B   Papifts

Papifts will fight in defence of the Proteftant Religion.

2. They are very fimple , that expect any care of the true Religion from the Prelates and their party, who have beene the grand perfecuters of it.

3. Neither is it to be imagined , that men fo loofe, lewd, and wicked, as moft of your Cavaliers are, fhould really intend the prefervation of Religion, or any thing elfe that is good.

4 We know the Earl of *Newcaftle* pretends that he fight for Religion, yet his Army is for the moft part Popifh, and he faid not long fince, That men might talk of Religion, and fo forth, but Religion of it felfe was but an ayerie thing.

5. Their rage and madneffe againft thofe that they know to have been moft zealous and forward in the maintenance and profeffion of the Proteftant Religion, doth fufficiently fhew how cordially they ftand for Religion.

6. Indeed they do ftand for Religion, but juft as the Ephefians ftood for *Diana*, Acts 17.

1. They ftand for a Popifh Prelacie.

2. They ftand for an Ignominious Clergie.

3. They ftand for the foule-ftarving Service-Booke.

4. They ftand for a companie of ftinking Ceremonies.

5. They ftand for abominable Monuments of Idolatrie.   6. They

6. They ftand for unchriftian liberty.

Q. *Do you think that there will be a Reformation of thefe things before we fhall injoy any peace?*

A. Yea doubtlefle : and I gather it from thefe Reafons.

1. Becaufe Gods anger is let loofe upon this Nation for thefe things.

2. Becaufe about this time hundred years Poperie was fuppreffed in this Kingdome ; and it is noted, that every Centurie, or hundred years, hath produced great alterations in the Church.

3. Becaufe it is Reformation that our Enemies do moft feare.

4. Becaufe the Devill and his Inftruments do fo beftirre themfelves at this time.

5. Becaufe all the reformed Churches in Chriftendome pray for and expect our Reformation.

6. Becaufe the meafure of our enemies iniquity is now full.

7. Becaufe a folemne Oath and Covenant is taken to that purpofe.

B 2   The

The Second Part of the Souldiers Catechifme.

Q. *WHat are the principall things requi-*
red in a Souldier?
    A. 1. That hee bee religious
and godly.

2. That he be couragious and valiant.

3. 3. That he be skilfull in the Militarie Profeffion.

Q. *How do you prove that our fouldiers fhould
be religious?*

A. 1. By Scripture : *Deut.23.9.Luk.3.14.*

2. Befides, there be many Reafons to con-
firme it.

1. Becaufe they lie fo open to death.

2. They ftand in continuall need of Gods affiftance.

3. They fight for Religion and Reformation.

4. God hath rais'd them up to execute juftice.

5. Men may be as religious in this Profeffion
as in any other.

6. We read of brave fouldiers that have been
very religious.

7. A well ordered Camp is a Schoole of Vertue,

tue, wherein is taught, 1. Preparation to death,
2. Continencie, 3. Vigilancie, 4. Obedience,
5. Hardnesse, 6. Temperance, 7. Humilitie,
8. Devotion, &c.

Q. *Who do chiefly offend against this Rule?*

A. 1. Such fouldiers as give themselves to whoring and uncleannesse.

2. Such as use to sweare, and blaspheme the name of God.

3. Such as follow that swinish sin of drunkennesse.

4. Such as plunder and steale whatsoever they come neare.

Q. *Are not thefe things tolerable in fouldiers?*

A. No more in them then other men: the Scripture faith generally to and of all men whatfoever:

1. That whoremongers and adulterers God will judge, *Heb.* 13.5.

2. That the Lord will not hold him guiltlesse that taketh his Name in vaine.

3. That drunkards shall not inherit the Kingdome of God, 1 *Cor.* 6.9,10.

4. That he that doth wrong, shall receive for the wrong he hath done, and there is no refpect of perfons, *Col.* 3.ult.

Q. *What is the reafon then that there be fo many lewd and Wicked men in the Parliaments Army?*

B 3

A. 1. Be

A. 1. Becaufe Commanders in Chief are not more carefull in choofing godly Officers.

2. Becaufe honeft religious men are not more forward to put forth themfelves in this fervice of God and his Church.

3. Becaufe Order and Difcipline is not more ftrictly executed by Superiours.

4. Becaufe Officers in Towns and Countries aim to preffe the fcumme and refufe of men, and fo by eafing themfelves, pefture our Armies with bafe conditioned people.

Q. How can we expect a bleffing upon our preparations, when fo many godleffe wretches are imployed in our Armies?

A. 1. Truly it is a very fad thing, and much to be lamented, and requires the care of the State to remedy.

2. Yet (bleffed be God) we have multitudes of godly and eminent Chriftians that are ingaged in the Parliaments Service.

3. And befides, we know that God can make ufe of wicked men to ferve his providence, as he doth of wicked Angells.

4. We have many inftances of bad men that have done good fervice to God and his Church, as *Saul, Ioab, &c.*

Q. Is it well done of fome of your Souldiers (which feem to be religious) to break down Croffes and Images where they meet with any?

A. 1. I

A. 1. I confesse that nothing ought to be done in a tumultuous manner.

2. But seeing God hath put the Sword of Reformation into the Souldiers hand, I thinke it is not amisse that they should cancell and demolish those Monuments of Superstition and Idolatry, especially seeing the Magistrate and the Minister that should have done it formerly, neglected it.

Q. But what say you to their tearing and burning the Books of Common Prayer, in every place where they come?

A. Much may be said in their iustification, who shew themselves so zealous against that Booke.

1. It hath been the fomenter of a most lazie lewd, and ignorant Ministry.

2. It hath been the Nurse of that lamentable blindnesse and ignorance, which hath overspread many parts of this Kingdome.

3. It is a great cause of our present calamities, for who are they that side with our Popish Enemies, but Common-Prayer men?

4. It is become the most abominable Idoll in the Land, people generally doe doat upon it, as much as the Ephesians upon *Diana* · and preferre it before Preaching in many places, being strangely inraged for the want of it.

5. It is high time therefore to remove this

Brazen

Brazen Serpent, and grinde it to powder, seeing it is the occasion of so much evill.

6. It is very likely therefore that God hath stirred up the spirits of some honest souldiers to be his Instruments for the destruction of that Idoll.

7. It belongs to the Parliament Souldiers, upon the matter, to remove all scandalous things they meet with, having covenanted, and ingaged themselves in the work of Reformation.

Q. *What doe you say concerning valour and courage?*

A. 1. I say, it is a most noble and heroicall vertue, that makes some men differ from others, as much as all men differ from beasts.

2. I say, it is impossible for any to be a good souldier without it. An Army of Harts led by a Lion, is better then an Army of Lions led by a Hart.

3. I say, that one valiant man in an Army, is better then a thousand cowards.

4. I say, that a coward degenerates from man, being of a base and ignoble nature.

1. God took speciall care, that all faint-hearted cowards should be cashiered out of his Armies, *Deut.* 20. 8.

2. Cowards ever do more hurt then good, being like an X before an L.

3. And for the most part cowards miscarrie
sooner

sooner then those that are couragious.

Q. *What are the chiefe Arguments and confi-derations to make a souldier couragious in the Parliaments Service?*

A. 1. The goodnesse of the Cause, which undoubtedly is Gods, and his Churches.

2. The promise of God, to help his Church and People against his and his Churches Enemies.

3. The manifold experiences that the people of God have had in former ages of his assistance.

4. The manifold experiences of Gods speciall odnesse to his servants in these times.

5. The assurance, that not a haire can fall from our heads without the providence and permission of God.

6. The danger of faint-heartednesse; he that would save his life in such times as these, shall lose it.

7. The promise, that whosoever shall lose his life, or any thing els, in the Cause of Christ and his Gospell, shall be a great gainer by the hand.

8. The consideration that this Warre is surrounded with the prayers and blessings of all the good people of the Land.

9. The multitude of eminent Christians, of all sorts, that are ingaged in this businesse.

10. The great reward of honour here, and glory hereafter, that shall be given to every one
that

that is valiant for the Lord.

Q. *What are the principall enemies to courage and valour?*

A. 1. Want of experience: fresh-water souldiers are commonly faint-hearted souldiers; whereas they that have been used to the Warres are usually of undaunted spirits.

2. Want of metall: some mens spirits are naturally so low and base, that they will never prove good souldiers: as it is with cocks, so is it amongst men: there is a breed and generation of cravens.

3. Want of Faith: when a man hath little or no confidence in God, his heart must needs faile him in undertakings of danger; whereas Faith feares not in the valley of the shadow of death. *Psal.*23.4

4. Want of innocency, and a good conscience, *Prov.*28.1. It was the speech of the valorous Earle of *Essex*, our renowned Generals Father, (cited by D. *Barlow* in his Sermon at *Pauls* Crosse, *March* 1.1600) That somtimes in the field encountering the enemy, the weight of his sinnesl ing heavie upon his conscience, being not reconciled to God quelled his spirits, and made him the most timerous man that might be.

5. Want of wisdome and consideration: for surely if men would seriously consider the evills

of

of cowardice, and the excellency of valour, it would make them abhorre the one, and be ambitious of the other.

Q. *Is there any great need of skill and cunning in this Profeffion?*

A. Yea doubtleffe : for *David* doth thankfully acknowledge the Lords goodnes, in teaching his hands to warre, and his fingers to fight, *Pfal.*144.1.

1. Great wifdome, policie, and experience is required in Commanders.

2. And no leffe skill and dexterity in common fouldiers ; they muft know how to handle their Armes, how to keep Ranks, &c.

3. Certainly a few well-trained Souldiers are better then a multitude of raw, unexperienced men.

Q. *What fhould be done to make fouldiers skilfull in their art ?*

A. 1. Officers fhould bee very diligent in teaching and exercifing their men.

2. Common fouldiers fhould make it their bufineffe to learn and get what cunning they can.

3. Every fouldier fhould feeke to God by prayer, that he would inftruct and teach them : for it is the bleffing of God that makes men to profit in any profeffion.

4. Both Commanders, Officers, and common Souldiers may advantage themfelves by

reading

reading and obferving what hath been written by eminent Souldiers, of this Act.

Q. *How ought Commanders and Officers to carry themfelves towards their Souldiers ?*

A. 1. Religioufly, fhewing them no evill example, but being a patterne to them of virtue and godlineffe.

2. Lovingly, not in a fterne rugged manner, confidering that their Command is not over Beares, But men.

3. Difcreetly, incouraging them moft that deferve beft, and avoiding fo much familiarity as may breed contempt.

4. Juftly, not defrauding them of their due, nor doing or fuffering any injury to be done to the meaneft.

Q. *How fhould inferiour Souldiers demeane themfelves toward their Commanders and Officers?*

A. 1. They muft acknowledge and honour them as Superiours, and account them as men fet over them by the providence of God and wifdome of the State.

2. They muft be exactly obedient to their command, even for confcience fake. *Rom.* 13. 5. of all men Souldiers are moft ftrictly tyed to obedience, the want whereof may prove of very dangerous confequence.

Q. *What fay you of fuch Souldiers as are given to mutining ?*   A. 1. They

A. 1. They are as dangerous Cattle as can belong to an Army.

2. They deserve severe punishment, and to be utterly cashiered.

3. They will hardly ever prove good Souldiers that are taynted with this humour.

Q. What is your opinion of those Souldiers that run away from their Colours?

A. 1. Such are, by Martiall Law, to suffer death, and surely, they well deserve it.

2. 'Tis a most ignoble and base part to doe so, and they deserve to be branded with infamy for ever, that are guilty of it.

3. Nay it is a fowle wickednesse, being offensive both to God and man, *Psal.* 78. 9.

1. For such (if the Cause be just) doe abandon the Cause of God.

2. They deceive that trust which was reposed in them by the State.

3. As much as in them lies, they betray the Cause they have undertaken.

4. They give dangerous example, and may occasion the overthrow of an Army.

Q. How ought souldiers to be incouraged and rewarded?

A. 1. They ought to be highly honoured, especially such as have been couragious and faithfull in their Countreyes Service.

2. They ought to be well maintained, with
sufficient

sufficient allowance, while they are abroad in imployment; for no man goeth on warfare at his own charges.

3. They that have received any hurt or losse by the warres, ought to be liberally provided for, and comfortably maintained all their dayes, by them that sent them forth.

Q. *What Arguments have you to prove, that such honour and respect should bee done to our souldiers?*

A. 1. They that fight against the Churches Enemies, are Gods helpers against the mighty, *Iudg.5.23.*

2. They are the Instruments of Justice, and the Executioners of Gods Judgements, *Psalme* 149.7,9.

3. They shew themselves men of publike spirits, and true lovers of their Countrey.

4. They shew themselves valiant and couragious, which are very high deserving qualities.

5 No men undergoe such hardship and hazzard as the souldier doth.

6. None deserve better then they, either of Church, Commonwealth, or Posterity.

F I N I S.

Printed in the USA
CPSIA information can be obtained
at www.ICGtesting.com
LVHW042259161124
796641LV00007B/121

* 9 7 8 1 1 6 1 6 9 0 2 0 0 *